99 Amazing Books and Films
Inspired by the Bible

B

museum of the Bible

BOOKS

Executive Editorial Team
Allen Quine
Wayne Hastings
Jeana Ledbetter
Byron Williamson

Managing Editor
Christopher D. Hudson

**Developmental
Editorial Team**
Tricia Drevets
Peggy Harvey
Andrew Klosterman
Brent McCulley
Laurence Paul
Melissa Peitsch
Daniel Reeves
Brad Spencer
Paula Stiles
Jennifer Turner
Len Woods

Worthy Editorial
Kyle Olund
Leeanna Nelson

Design & Page Layout
Mark Wainwright,
Symbology Creative

Cover Design
Matt Smartt,
Smartt Guys design

Cover Art
Charles Bowman /
Alamy Stock Photo

99 Amazing Books and Films Inspired by the Bible,
© 2017 Museum of the Bible, Inc.
Published by Worthy Publishing Group, a division of Worthy Media, Inc. in association with Museum of the Bible.

ISBN-10: 194547002X
ISBN-13: 978-1945470028

Library of Congress Control Number: 2017949577

Produced with the assistance of Hudson Bible.

Printed in the USA

1 2 3 4 5 6 7 8 9 LBM 22 21 20 19 18 17

ALAMY • Advertising Archives/Alamy: 39, 88 • AF archive/Alamy: pages 20, 22, 29, 52, 53, 63, 72, 81, 108, 109 • Alamy: 9, 17, 23, 54, 69, 77, 83, 95, 98 • Alpha Historica/Alamy: 37 • capt.digby/Alamy: 35 • CBW/Alamy: 11 • dmac/Alamy: 37 • dpa picture alliance/Alamy: 40 • Entertainment Pictures/Alamy: 41, 79, 86, 97, 111 • Glasshouse Images/Alamy: 24 • IanDagnall Computing/Alamy: 8 • INTERFOTO/Alamy: 42 • Lebrecht Music and Arts Photo Library/Alamy: 50,62 • Moviestore Collection/Alamy: 25, 27, 58, 61, 66, 70, 71, 75, 77, 89, 101, 102 • Old Paper Studios/Alamy: 12 • Photo12/Alamy 10, 21, 33, 38, 47, 69, 85 • Pictorial Press LTD/Alamy 18, 19, 74, 76, 84, 56 • Ronald Grant Archive/Alamy: 26, 43, 89 • ScreenProd / Photononstop/Alamy: 16 • ScreenProd/Alamy: 105 • Silver Screen/Alamy: 14, 18 • SVENSK FILMINDUSTRI / Ronald Grant Archive/Alamy: 44 • United Archives GmbH/Alamy 39, 45 • World History Archive/Alamy   EVERETT • Buena Vista Pictures/courtesy Everett Collection: 73 • Century-Fox Film Corp /Everett Collection : 24, 81 • Columbia Pictures/courtesy Everett Collection: 30 • DreamWorks/courtesy Everett Collection: 103 • Everett Collection: 14, 31, 40, 42, 46, 48, 49, 51, 54, 55, 59, 67, 68, 74, 84, 91, 93, 94, 96, 99, 107, 110 • Mary Evans/Ronald Grant/Everett Collection: 70 • New Yorker Films/courtesy Everett Collection: 28 • Paramount Pictures/ Courtesy: Everett Collection: 31, 78, 80, 102 • Ronald Grant/Everett Collection: 49, 97, 99 • Samuel Goldwyn/Everett Collection: 104 • TriStar Pictures/Courtesy Everett Collection: 86 • United Artists/Everett Collection: 92 • Universal/courtesy Everett Collection: 106 • Walt Disney/courtesy Everett Collection: 88 • Warner Bros/Everett Collection: 50, 57, 82, 95   ISTOCKPHOTO • Bluejayphoto/istockphoto: 24 • Duncan1890/istockphoto: 34   COMMONS WIKIMEDIA • 21, 34, 55, 60, 63, 103   SHUTTERSTOCK • Alexey V Smirnov/Shutterstock: 62 • BHammond/Shutterstock: 96 • Bjoern Wylezich/shutterstock: 22 • Boris Stroujko/Shutterstock: 8 • Claudio Divizia/shutterstock: 15 • Denis Belitsky/shutterstock: 87 • Fernando Cortes/shutterstock: 60 • Infrequent_Flyer/shutterstock: 64 • InnaVar/shutterstock: 13 • Joseph Sohm/shutterstock: 80 • Jurik Peter/shutterstock: 87 • R-O-M-A/shutterstock: 20 • Richard Cavalleri/shutterstock: 9 • Shane Gross/shutterstock: 10 • shutterstock: 44 • Suchota/Shutterstock: 15 • Yeryomina Anastassiya/shutterstock: 108 • Zastolskiy Victor/shutterstock: 65 • Columbia Pictures/Courtesy Everett Collection: 71 • Everett Historical/shutterstock: 36

museum of the Bible
BOOKS

WORTHY®
PUBLISHING

99 Amazing Books and Films Inspired by the Bible

Introduction

This book focuses on the Bible's impact on two powerful forms of sharing stories—books and film. In our vibrant world of ideas, writers and directors are often inspired by biblical stories and themes—including the Bible's rich array of drama, conflict, moral and ethical dilemmas, and universal questions about suffering and hope. Because of the global reach of books and film, people from all different cultures have opportunities to explore some of the most popular narratives inspired by biblical stories.

Biblical narratives and other literary works became more diverse and popular as the printing press increased the number of books in print. As a result, more people gained exposure to rich literary fare. Then, in the nineteenth and twentieth centuries, with the advent of photography and the subsequent development of moving pictures, a new form of storytelling—including stories inspired by the Bible—with mass audiences became possible. By the 1920s, films became widely accessible and affordable.

As you will discover in *99 Amazing Books and Films Inspired by the Bible*, some of the highlighted books and films attempt to represent biblical events as they might have occurred. Others portray biblical themes rather than biblical events. Still other books and films depict historical figures who were inspired by the Bible to live in heroic ways.

Whether you are an avid reader or a film connoisseur, this book can serve as a guide for anyone interested in knowing more about the Bible's impact on literature and film.

01

The Divine Comedy
Dante Alighieri

***Dante's epic poem* The Divine Comedy** is recognized as a towering achievement in Western literature. The work, an exploration of the afterlife of the damned, is suffused with biblical imagery.

Dante imagines hell as an enormous funnel that leads to the center of the earth. According to Dante, the funnel was created when God threw Satan and his angels out of heaven (compare Isaiah 14:12). Dante's tour of hell, led by the ancient poet Virgil, begins in the vestibule—that is, the layer or circle nearest the surface of the earth. Here the uncommitted are tormented by insects that bite.

As Dante descends deeper into hell, he encounters nine circles. Each successive circle contains souls whose sins were more egregious (in Dante's opinion) than the last—and whose corresponding punishments are more severe.

The deepest pit of Dante's ninth circle of hell is reserved for Satan and the three most despicable human traitors who ever lived: Brutus and Cassius, the Roman senators who conspired to kill Julius Caesar, and Judas Iscariot, whose betrayal of Jesus Christ is recorded in Luke 22. ∎

Left: *Dante and the Divine Comedy* by Domenico di Michelino (1417–1491).

02 Frankenstein
Mary Shelley

Frankenstein *is a story of creation and of the relationship between the creature and the creator.* The characters in Mary Shelley's novel—especially the creature—are acutely aware of the parallels between their story and the Bible's account of creation. The monster in Mary Shelley's novel is much different from the monosyllabic brute portrayed by Boris Karloff in the 1931 film. Shelley's creature is capable of complex thought and eloquent communication.

Perhaps the most pointed Bible reference in the novel comes from the monster, who says to Victor Frankenstein, his creator, "Remember that I am thy creature; I ought to be thy Adam." His loneliness and frustration are palpable. He feels neglected by his creator, denied the one thing he needs to live a fulfilling life: a mate, such as the one God provided for Adam as recorded in the Genesis account of creation.

Victor's refusal to provide a mate drives the creature to deadly revenge. His monstrous acts cause him to recognize similarities between himself and another created being who figures prominently in the book of Genesis—Satan. ∎

Above Left: Illustration by Theodore von Holst (1810–1844) in the 3rd edition of *Frankenstein* (1831) by Mary Shelley (1797–1851).
Above Right: Castle Frankenstein, Germany.

03

The Scarlet Letter: A Romance

Nathaniel Hawthorne

Literary scholars have identified more than three dozen allusions to the Bible in *The Scarlet Letter*, Hawthorne's classic tale of sin, guilt, and repentance. The allusions begin with the scarlet letter of the title—*A* stands for adultery. The adulterous affair between Hester Prynne and Arthur Dimmesdale is central to the novel's plot. The color of the letter is drawn from the book of Isaiah, which says, "Though your sins are like scarlet, they shall be as white as snow" (1:18).

In contrasting Reverend Dimmesdale with the other Puritan clergy of that time and place, Hawthorne notes that Dimmesdale possessed what the others did not: the tongues of fire that descended on Jesus's followers at Pentecost (Acts 2:3)—that is, the ability to communicate effectively in "the heart's native language."

Hester names her daughter Pearl in reference to the "pearl of great value" from Jesus's parable recorded in Matthew 13:45–46.

Perhaps the most significant biblical allusion in Hawthorne's masterwork involves the Genesis story of Adam and Eve in the garden of Eden. Because of their sin, Hester and Dimmesdale are expelled from the good graces of their community as Adam and Eve were expelled from Eden. ■

Above Right: *The Century* (1912) by Sigismond de Ivanowski (1875–1944).
Above Left: The House of the Seven Gables, Salem, Massachusetts (1668). Famous from *The Scarlet Letter* (1851) by Nathaniel Hawthorne (1804–1864).

04

Moby-Dick; or, The Whale
Herman Melville

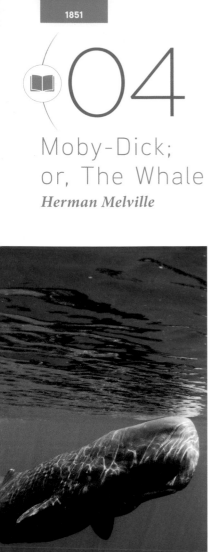

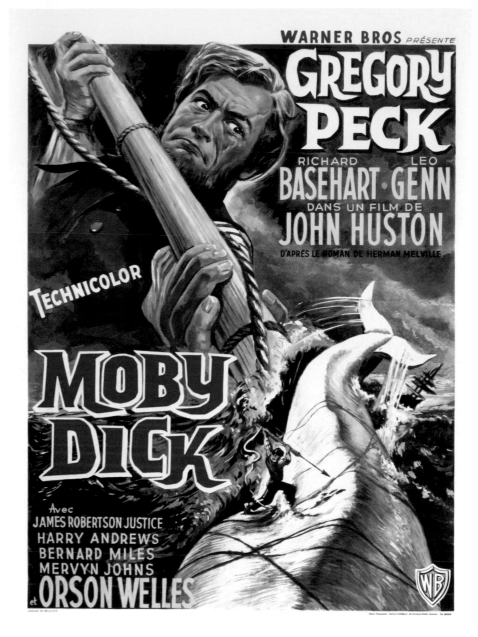

Herman Melville's seafaring classic tells the story of Captain Ahab and his relentless pursuit of Moby-Dick, the white whale that took his leg.

The biblical allusions in *Moby-Dick* begin with the novel's iconic opening line: "Call me Ishmael." Ishmael is the narrator of Melville's story, the only one left alive at the end to tell the tale. His name comes from the book of Genesis (16:11). Ishmael was Abraham's firstborn son, the product of the patriarch's misguided liaison with his wife's handmaid. The Bible portrays Ishmael as an outcast. He ceased to be his father's favorite when Abraham's wife Sarah gave birth to a son (Isaac). He was fated to a life of wandering when his father turned him and his mother away. His name is apt for Melville's narrator, a young man whose wanderlust leads him to the whaling ship *Pequod*.

Before they sign up for the voyage, Ishmael and his future shipmate Queequeg attend a church service. The sermon topic? Jonah—the prophet who ran away to sea and was swallowed by a great fish.

An eccentric named Elijah warns that tragedy will ensue if Ishmael and Queequeg cast off with Ahab. His prediction recalls the enmity recorded in the Bible between the prophet Elijah and King Ahab of Israel.

Allusions to the Bible continue throughout the novel, with references to Lazarus, Canaan, the Philistines, and Job, to name a few. ∎

Above Right: *Moby Dick* original movie poster (1956).
Above Left: Sperm whale off the coast of Sri Lanka.

05 The Sound and the Fury
William Faulkner

William Faulkner's story of the downfall and ruin of the aristocratic Compson family is told in four parts—each is related by a different narrator, set on a specific day in the family's history, and tinged with a prominent biblical theme.

The first section of *The Sound and the Fury* is narrated by Benjy, the Compsons' thirty-three-year-old autistic son. Benjy recalls his grandmother's funeral, held at the family estate. Benjy and his siblings are sent outside and told to stay away from the house during the funeral. Caddy, Benjy's sister, climbs a tree to see what's going on inside. The image of Caddy gaining forbidden knowledge by way of a tree recalls Eve's temptation in the garden of Eden. The point is driven home when Dilsey, the Compsons' maid, spies Caddy, calls her "Satan," and tells her to climb out of the tree.

The second section is narrated by Quentin, the Compsons' oldest son. He recalls an event that occurred on Maundy Thursday, the day on which some Christians commemorate Jesus's last meal with his disciples (Matthew 26:26–30). In this section, Quentin partakes of a kind of Christian communion as he drinks wine during a picnic with friends and later breaks bread with a young Italian girl.

The third section, narrated by Dilsey, the Compsons' second-oldest son, is set on Good Friday, the day many Christians commemorate Jesus's crucifixion. In the

The Sound and the Fury (1929) by William Faulkner (1897–1962).

06 Superman Comic Books
Jerry Siegel and Joe Shuster

As teenagers in Cleveland, Ohio, in the early 1930s, writer Jerry Siegel and artist Joe Shuster created the iconic superhero Superman. Siegel and Shuster came from Jewish immigrant families, which may explain the echoes of Moses's story in Superman's origins.

The Hebrew Bible records that as a baby, Moses was bundled into a watertight basket and sent off alone by his mother in order to save him (Exodus 2). As a baby, Superman was bundled into a spaceship and sent off alone by his father in order to save him.

As the mythology of Superman developed over the decades, however, allusions to another Bible character became more pronounced: Jesus.

In the guise of mild-mannered reporter Clark Kent, Superman avoids recognition by blending in with the people he came to help. According to the Gospels, Jesus was raised by commoners, grew up in a contemptible town (John 1:46), worked as a carpenter (Mark 6:3), and surrounded himself with working-class people (Matthew 4:18–22).

Superman communicates with and draws strength from his father in his Fortress of Solitude. Compare that to Mark 1:35: "And rising very early in the morning, while it was still dark, he departed and went out to a desolate place, and there he prayed."

The allusions to Jesus reached their climax in 1993 when DC Comics stunned the graphic-novel world by killing off Superman. The Man of Steel died saving humanity from a seemingly unstoppable killing machine named Doomsday.

In the wake of the Man of Steel's death, false Supermen arise. Compare that to Jesus's prophecy concerning his death, recorded in Matthew 24:24: "For false christs and false prophets will arise and perform great signs and wonders, so as to lead astray." The comparisons to Jesus conclude with Superman's resurrection. ∎

Top: Action Comics #61 featuring Superman, by DC Comics (June 1943).

07 The Hobbit and The Lord of the Rings

J. R. R. Tolkien

J. R. R. Tolkien's The Hobbit *and epic three-volume* The Lord of the Rings series are infused with powerful biblical themes—despite the absence of direct references to God, the Bible, or Jesus.

Many readers have identified with the band of hapless diminutive hobbits who embark upon adventures in Middle-earth in a quest to find and destroy a mysterious Ring that is infused with diabolical powers. The Ring is said to be a symbol of original sin, or the first sin of Adam and Eve in the garden of Eden (Genesis 3:6). Tolkien's intricate geography presented in the novels has been meticulously mapped by aficionados, and it symbolizes spiritual dualism. The East is a vast dark region ruled by malevolent creatures, while goodness is found in the West, culminating in the Undying Lands beyond the Great Sea.

The hobbits encounter fantastical beings that some believe are analogous to Satan and his demons, as described in the Bible, including the fearsome dragon Smaug and the Dark Lord Sauron, who is finally confronted in a climactic battle.

The hobbits receive critical assistance from an eccentric cast of characters, led by the wizard Gandalf, commander of the Army of the West. Numerous commentators have viewed Gandalf as a messianic figure who gives his life to save his companions and save Middle-earth from the nefarious powers. Brought back to life, Gandalf the White defeats Sauron, and the Ring is finally destroyed by fire deep within Mount Doom.

With more than 250 million copies sold, Tolkien's novels are among the best-selling books of all time. ■

Below: The film set for *The Hobbit* and *The Lord of the Rings* trilogy from the rolling green hills of Matamata in the North Island of New Zealand.

08 It Happened One Night

Anyone familiar with the screwball comedies of the 1930s and 1940s will recognize the story arc of *It Happened One Night*: The bickering, mismatched antagonists come to see each other in a different light. Though circumstances and misunderstandings threaten to keep them apart, in the end they discover they were meant for each other.

Likewise, anyone familiar with the biblical narrative of Joshua 6 knows what happened to the walls of Jericho: the Israelite priests blew their trumpets and shouted, and the barrier collapsed. The creators of *It Happened One Night* drew on that well-known Bible story for an unforgettable final scene.

On their honeymoon, Warne and Ellie return to the auto-camp cabin. The manager of the auto-camp and his wife discuss the strange requests of the newlywed couple: a rope, a blanket, and a toy trumpet. The movie ends with the sound of the trumpet being blown and a shot of a blanket falling to the floor.

It Happened One Night is one of only three movies to sweep the five major Academy Award categories: Best Picture, Best Actor, Best Actress, Best Director, and Best Adaptation. It is ranked number 35 on the American Film Institute's list of the one hundred greatest American movies. ∎

In the film It Happened One Night, out-of-work reporter Peter Warne stumbles onto the biggest story of his career when he discovers runaway celebrity heiress Ellie Andrews on a bus. Ellie is traveling to New York to reunite with her husband, whom she married against her father's wishes. Her wealthy and powerful father has dispatched detectives to find her and bring her back to him. Warne agrees to escort Ellie to New York in exchange for the exclusive rights to her story.

To avoid detection, the two travel by bus from Miami to the Big Apple. At one point, they pose as a married couple in order to spend the night in an auto-camp cabin. Though the room has separate beds, Ellie is understandably suspicious of Warne's motives. But Warne has noble intentions, and to prove it he strings a clothesline between the two beds and hangs a blanket over it to create a barrier. He calls it the "walls of Jericho." He is alluding to the ancient city of Jericho, which, according to the Bible, was protected by impenetrable walls (Joshua 6).

Above: *It Happened One Night* original movie poster (1934).
Right: Clark Gable and Claudette Colbert in the film *It Happened One Night* (1934).

Hamlet

William Shakespeare

Like many of Shakespeare's best-known works, *Hamlet*, the story of a prince's thirst for revenge on the uncle who killed his father and seized the throne of Denmark, contains several references to the Bible.

In act 1, scene 1, Hamlet's friend Horatio reports seeing the ghost of Hamlet's father, but he notes that the ghost disappeared when the cock crowed. In response, the sentry Marcellus refers to the Advent story ("that season comes wherein our Savior's birth is celebrated") in explaining the legend that in the days before Christmas, cocks crow all day long to keep ghosts away.

In act 1, scene 3, Hamlet evokes Jesus's words recorded in Matthew 7:13–14 to assail clergy who fail to practice what they preach: "Do not, as some ungracious pastors do, show me the steep and thorny way to heaven, whilst, like a puff'd and reckless libertine, himself the primrose path of dalliance treads."

In act 1, scene 4, Hamlet's father's description of his spiritual dwelling place—"confin'd to fast in fires"—is reminiscent of the abode of the rich man in Jesus's parable of the rich man and Lazarus recorded in Luke 16.

In act 2, scene 2, Hamlet reveals his high opinion of human nature by referencing Genesis 1:27 ("So God created man in his own image") in his conversation with his friends Rosencrantz and Guildenstern: "What a piece of work is a man! how noble in reason! how infinite in faculties! in form and moving how express and admirable! in action how like an angel! in apprehension how like a god!" ∎

Right: Statue of William Shakespeare (1874) in Leicester Square, London, UK.

10 Sergeant York

Sergeant York *tells the true story of Alvin York,* one of the most decorated American soldiers in World War I. The movie introduces York in 1916 as a hard-drinking, ne'er-do-well hillbilly from Tennessee who changes his ways when he falls in love with a young woman named Gracie. However, when his plan to buy a plot of land to settle and farm is spoiled by a romantic rival, York goes looking for revenge.

In a scene reminiscent of Saul's encounter with a blinding light, recorded in Acts 9, York is struck by a bolt of lightning. Dazed, he wanders into a nearby church, where a service is underway. To the strains of "Give Me That Old Time Religion," York renounces violence and vows to live his life according to the Bible's teachings.

When he is drafted for World War I, York tries to claim conscientious objector status, but he is denied. He reports to boot camp and explains his position to his commanding officers. One of them, a captain, engages him in debate. In a fascinating scene, the two men take turns quoting Bible passages to each other as they lay out their opposing viewpoints. The other officer, a major, hands York a history book and reminds him that many great Americans have given their all for their country. The major gives York ten days to return to Tennessee to sort through his beliefs.

Back in his home state, York finds solitude on a rock ledge. With the history book and his Bible, he tries to answer the question of whether God or country should come first in a person's life. His epiphany comes when a gust of wind blows open his Bible to these words of Jesus: "Render to Caesar the things that are Caesar's, and to God the things that are God's" (Mark 12:17).

His conscience at ease, York returns to his unit. When he finally sees combat on the French front, York single-handedly kills twenty German soldiers—and then, with a handful of other Americans, captures 132 more. He is awarded virtually every military honor for his heroics.

Gary Cooper was awarded an Academy Award for Best Actor for his portrayal of York. The movie proved to be wildly successful with 1941 audiences, who saw the specter of another war to end all wars growing on the horizon. While the film was in theaters, the Japanese bombed Pearl Harbor. ∎

Top: Gary Cooper in the film *Sergeant York* (1941).

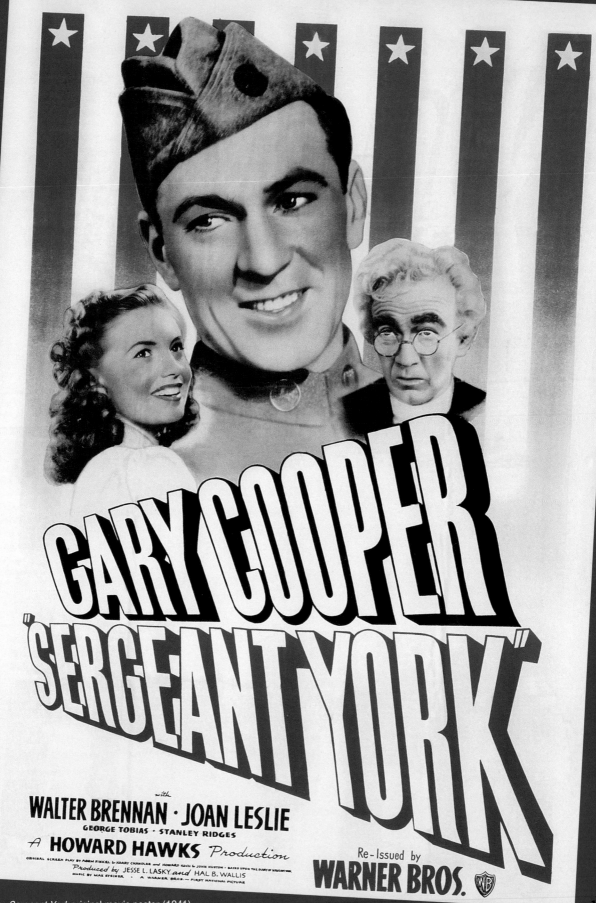

Above: *Sergeant York* original movie poster (1941).

11 Samson and Delilah

Famed director Cecil B. DeMille was no stranger to biblical epics. He had mounted a silent production of *The Ten Commandments* as early as 1923. The movie was a hit, and DeMille was convinced there was an audience for more Bible-based blockbusters, which he infused with an odd mixture of reverence and sex appeal.

The doomed romance of Samson and Delilah seemed like the perfect vehicle for one of DeMille's ventures into the Bible. He started preproduction on the project in 1935 but then set it aside for well over a decade. Casting proved to be a challenge. Dozens of Hollywood's leading ladies were considered for Delilah before DeMille settled on Hedy Lamarr. Burt Lancaster was the director's first choice for Samson, but a bad back forced him out. Victor Mature stepped in as his replacement.

The film version of Samson and Delilah's story covers all the expected highlights:

- Samson's Nazirite vows that prohibited him from cutting his hair—which, in turn, gave him supernatural strength
- Delilah's devious manipulation to discover Samson's secret
- The spectacular conclusion involving the collapse of the Philistine temple

The screenwriters took certain liberties with the story for dramatic effect. In the film, unlike in the Bible, it is Delilah who leads the blinded Samson to the temple pillars—and who stays behind to die with her people when Samson pushes down the pillars, causing the entire structure to collapse and killing everyone inside.

The film proved to be a hit with filmgoers. *Samson and Delilah* was the highest-grossing movie of 1950. When its initial run ended, it was the third highest grossing movie of all time. ∎

Left: Hedy Lamarr in the Paramount film *Samson and Delilah* (1949).
Above: *Samson and Delilah* original movie poster (1949).

12 The Night of the Hunter

In **The Night of the Hunter,** a man on the run after a robbery turns deadly hides ten thousand dollars in his daughter's doll and makes his two young children, John and Pearl, promise that they will never tell anyone where the money is. The man is arrested, but before he is executed, he inadvertently reveals to his cellmate that he hid the money with his children.

That cellmate, locked up for stealing a car, is a psychopath named Harry Powell, who poses as a preacher in order to court, wed, and ultimately murder unsuspecting widows for their money. After his parole, he sets his sights on his cellmate's widow—and especially her children—in order to discover where the money is hidden.

After Powell murders their mother, John and Pearl escape (with the doll) by floating downstream on a skiff. In a scene reminiscent of the Hebrew Bible's story of the baby Moses being pulled from the Nile, the two innocents are discovered and taken in by a kindly old woman named Rachel Cooper. Rachel and Powell, who has followed the children, engage in a game of cat and mouse, as she tries to protect them and he tries to harm them to get the money.

In contrast to the plot, the rhythm, the look, and the characterizations of *The Night of the Hunter* are anything but conventional.

The Bible plays a key role in establishing the characters of Powell and Rachel. Powell uses Bible verses as weapons and justifications for his evil nature. His God is one of violence and hate. He sees his murder spree as God's work, suggesting in a prayer that he and God share a love of killing and a hatred of "frilly things." He quotes Proverbs 23:27: "A strange woman is a narrow pit" (KJV).

Regarding the switchblade he carries, the preacher quotes Jesus's words in Matthew 10:34: "I came not to send peace, but a sword" (KJV). When the children resist his efforts to get them to tell him where the money is, he paraphrases Proverbs 6:16–17 by saying, "A liar is an abomination before mine eyes."

Rachel's knowledge of the Bible shows her to be a loving, no-nonsense protector who can see through Powell's lies. Her use of Matthew 7:18–20 is especially apt: "A good tree cannot bring forth evil fruit, neither can a corrupt tree bring forth good fruit. . . . Wherefore by their fruits ye shall know them" (KJV).

Though it was a critical and commercial flop when it was released, *The Night of the Hunter* has grown in stature over the years and is acknowledged as an influence on such filmmaking giants as Martin Scorsese, Terrence Malick, and the Coen brothers. ■

13 The Ten Commandments

After the box-office success of 1949's Samson and Delilah, director Cecil B. DeMille determined to up the ante for his next—and final—biblical epic. He chose as his subject matter the story of Moses, the adopted Egyptian prince who, according to the Hebrew Bible, discovers his Hebrew heritage and eventually leads his people out of slavery in Egypt.

The result was his 1956 production of *The Ten Commandments*—the biblical epic against which all others are measured. DeMille filmed his magnum opus on location in Egypt and throughout the Sinai Peninsula. The special effects—state of the art in the 1950s—still impress today. The iconic scene in which Moses parts the Red Sea is considered one of the greatest visual effects in movie history.

DeMille's film is relatively faithful to the Bible's account of the Exodus, though dramatic license is taken throughout. The relationship between Moses and his adopted royal family of Egypt, especially his rivalry with his half brother Rameses II, adds emotional heft to the film but is entirely the invention of the film's screenwriters.

The Ten Commandments was nominated for seven Academy Awards, including Best Picture. Adjusted for inflation, its box-office grosses place it seventh on the list of the most profitable movies ever made. ■

Top: Charlton Heston in the film *The Ten Commandments* (1956).
Above Right: Pyramids in Egypt.

14 Ben-Hur

Ben-Hur *is based on the 1880 novel* Ben-Hur: A Tale of the Christ by Lew Wallace, who served as a major general of Union forces during the American Civil War, governor of the New Mexico territory, and United States ambassador to Turkey. His book was not only the best-selling work of fiction in the nineteenth century but also used as an evangelism tool by Christian churches of the era.

The first film adaptation of Wallace's novel was released in 1925 as a silent feature. The latest was released in 2016. But it is the 1959 version that looms over Hollywood history. The film was awarded a record eleven Academy Awards, including Best Picture. It is ranked seventy-two on the American Film Institute's list of the one hundred greatest American movies ever made.

The film tells the story of Judah Ben-Hur (memorably portrayed by Charlton Heston), a wealthy merchant in Judea during the time of Christ who is betrayed by Messala, a childhood friend-turned-Roman tribune. Judah is condemned to a life of slavery in the Roman galleys, and his mother and sister are imprisoned.

With a group of other condemned men, Judah is marched through the desert. Along the way, the caravan passes through Nazareth, where a kind young man named Jesus gives Judah water that saves his life.

Years pass as Judah rows in the galleys of Roman ships, all the while plotting his revenge on Messala. His opportunity comes when he encounters an Arab sheik and a man named Balthasar, one of the "wise men" described in the Bible's Advent story who had brought gifts to the infant Jesus. Balthasar senses goodness in Judah and tells him about the now-adult Jesus. The sheik nurtures Judah's chariot-racing skills, giving him an opportunity to challenge Messala, who is also a skilled—and notorious—chariot racer.

The climactic chariot race in the arena is regarded as one of the greatest action sequences ever filmed. After several close encounters, Messala collides with another chariot and is dragged to his death by his own stampeding horses. Judah wins the race. Before Messala dies, though, he reveals that Judah's mother and sister aren't dead, as Judah believed. Instead, Messala had them sent to a leper colony.

Judah is able to rescue his now-leprous mother and sister. As they return to the city, they encounter Jesus, who is being led to his crucifixion. Judah recognizes Jesus as the young man who gave him water years earlier. When Jesus stumbles, Judah rushes to his aid to give him water.

Judah and his mother and sister follow Jesus to Golgotha, where they witness his crucifixion. At the moment of Jesus's death, Judah's mother and sister are healed of their leprosy. Judah returns to his home a changed man. ■

Top Right: Charlton Heston, from the trailer to the film *Ben-Hur*.
Right: Charlton Heston and Stephen Boyd in the film *Ben-Hur* (1959).

21

15 Elmer Gantry

***Elmer Gantry, in the film* Elmer Gantry,** is a traveling salesman who isn't above quoting Bible passages and feigning religious fervor to peddle his wares. He teams with a female evangelist named Sister Sharon Falconer (whose character is based on the disgraced Canadian evangelist Aimee Semple McPherson) to travel the small-town America tent-revival circuit in the 1920s.

His fire-and-brimstone sermons, followed by her messages of repentance and salvation, resonate with the spiritual seekers in their audience—people inclined to give generously to support "God's work." In time, Gantry and Sharon collect enough money to build the tabernacle that Sharon has always dreamed of.

Their partnership is thwarted by a former flame of Gantry's who ensnares him in a blackmail plot and ruins his reputation. Sharon, meanwhile, becomes convinced that she is a vessel of God's power. After she "heals" a deaf man at one of her services, a fire breaks out in the tabernacle. Gantry tries to save her, but Sharon rushes back into the flames and dies.

In the final scene of the movie, Sharon's business manager proposes that Gantry take over Sharon's ministry. Gantry smiles and enigmatically quotes 1 Corinthians 13:11: "When I was a child, I spake as a child, I understood as a child . . . when I became a man, I put away childish things" (KJV). And then he walks away. ∎

Above: Burt Lancaster in the film *Elmer Gantry* (1960).
Left: Antique Bible photographed by Bjoern Wylezich.

16

The Greatest Story Ever Told

In the early 1960s, director George Stevens, taking a page from Cecil B. DeMille's playbook, mounted his own lavish production of a Bible story for the ages. Using the New Testament Gospels as his source material, Stevens spared no expense in bringing the story of Jesus to the screen.

Stevens commissioned a French artist to create over 350 oil paintings to be used as storyboards. He tapped the poet Carl Sandburg to serve as a creative consultant on the project. He traveled to Rome to meet with Pope John XXIII before filming commenced. He shot over 1,100 miles of film that he condensed into a 260-minute running time.

The result is a reverent, highlights approach to the Gospel narrative. *The Greatest Story Ever Told* solemnly (some critics say too solemnly) re-creates Jesus's birth, his baptism, his sermons, his miracles, his relationship with his disciples, his arrest and trial, his crucifixion, and his resurrection, as recorded in the Bible.

For the role of Jesus (a Middle Eastern Jew), Stevens tapped then-unknown Swedish actor Max von Sydow. Stevens filled out the cast with an assortment of stars from the big screen (Charlton Heston and Claude Rains) and the small screen (Telly Savalas and Martin Landau). Because the movie was seen as a prestige picture, many of the biggest names in Hollywood agreed to cameo roles just to be a part of it.

That would explain why John Wayne appears as a Roman centurion at Jesus's crucifixion to deliver a single line (as only John Wayne could): "Truly this man was the Son of God!" (Mark 15:39). ∎

Right: Max von Sydow in the film *The Greatest Story Ever Told* (1965).

17 The Sound of Music

Perhaps the most beloved of all screen musicals, *The Sound of Music* is the story of Maria, a nun-turned-nanny who melts the heart of the cold and distant Captain von Trapp, the widowed father of a brood of preternaturally talented singing children. Based on a true story, the film is set in 1938 Austria, as the Nazis are beginning their rise to power.

As the movie builds to its dramatic conclusion, with the Nazis pursuing the von Trapp family, Maria leads the family back to her convent. There, the Mother Abbess urges them to flee for safety over the Alps by quoting Psalm 121:1: "I will lift up mine eyes unto the hills, from whence cometh my help" (KJV). ∎

Left: Julie Andrews in the film *The Sound of Music* (1965).

Above Right: *The Sound of Music* original movie poster (1965).

Above Left: Historic city of Salzburg, Austria, where *The Sound of Music* was filmed.

18 The Abominable Dr. Phibes

One of the strangest entries in the genre of movies inspired by the Bible is the 1971 minor horror classic *The Abominable Dr. Phibes*. Dr. Phibes, played by Vincent Price, is a mechanical genius and madman who is believed to have died in a car accident shortly after the death of his wife. In fact, Dr. Phibes is very much alive—though horribly disfigured—and exacting an elaborate revenge on the medical personnel he holds responsible for his wife's death.

The theme of his revenge is the ten plagues of Egypt, as recorded in Exodus 7–11. The plagues of Egypt were intended to soften the heart of Pharaoh so he would free the Hebrew slaves. Dr. Phibes uses the plagues for shock value as he dispatches them one by one on the surgical team that failed to save his wife. His murderous rampage involves (or makes reference to) boils, bees, frogs, blood, hail, and locusts.

Though his plan to kill the firstborn son of the head surgeon is thwarted at the last minute, Dr. Phibes escapes to fight another day—in the 1972 sequel, *Dr. Phibes Rises Again*. ∎

Top: Vincent Price (right) in the film *The Abominable Dr. Phibes* (1971).

19 Places in the Heart

Set in Depression-era Texas, *Places in the Heart* tells the story of Edna Spalding, a widow trying to save her family farm in the face of long odds. In addition to the forces of nature that threaten her cotton crop, Edna is forced to contend with an unsympathetic bank pressuring her to sell the farm and a violent strain of racism in her community that threatens those closest to her. Her allies are Moses ("Moze"), an African American handyman, and Mr. Will, a blind lodger.

Together, the group, along with some key helpers, manages to defy the odds and bring in the all-important first crop of the season. But there is a price to be paid for their success. Local Ku Klux Klan members, incensed by Moze's role as Edna's business partner, savagely beat Moze. Only the intervention of Mr. Will, who recognizes the voices of the hooded attackers, prevents Moze's death. With the threat of future attacks looming, Moze is forced to leave the farm for good.

In a highly symbolic coda filled with biblical imagery, the film's characters—black and white, living and dead—are shown gathered at the local church, sharing communion with one another. The preacher paraphrases 1 Corinthians 11:23–25, which says: "The Lord Jesus on the night when he was betrayed took bread, and when he had given thanks, he broke it, and said, 'This is my body, which is for you. Do this in remembrance of me.' In the same way also he took the cup, after supper, saying, 'This cup is the new covenant in my blood. Do this, as often as you drink it, in remembrance of me.' "

The scene brings to mind the description in Galatians 3:28: "There is neither Jew nor Greek, there is neither slave nor free, there is no male and female, for you are all one in Christ Jesus." ∎

Sally Field (middle right) and Danny Glover (far right) in the film *Places in the Heart* (1984).

20 Hoosiers

Based on the true story of a tiny Indiana high school basketball team's improbable run to the 1952 state championship, Hoosiers is one of the great sports underdog movies.

The movie traces the lives of the players, coaches, families, and fans in the tight-knit, basketball-crazy farming community of Hickory. It charts the ups and downs of one magical season as the team and their new coach learn to trust one another.

The movie builds to Hickory's showdown with the mighty South Bend Central Bears, a perennial Indiana basketball powerhouse. As the members of the seemingly overmatched Hickory team enjoy a moment of bonding and reflection in their locker room before the big game, the team chaplain steps forward to offer an invocation.

Without so much as a glance at his Bible, the chaplain prays this paraphrase of 1 Samuel 17:49: "And David put his hand in the bag and took out a stone and slung it. And it struck the Philistine on the head, and he fell to the ground. Amen."[1]

Duly inspired, the Hickory players take the court to slay their own giant. After a furious comeback, the team's star player hits a last-second shot to win the championship. ∎

Gene Hackman (center) in the film *Hoosiers* (1986).

21 Dekalog

Dekalog *is a collection of ten hour-long films* directed by Krzysztof Kieslowski that was broadcast as a miniseries on Polish television in 1989. Today it is regarded as one of the landmark achievements in world cinema.

As its name implies, *Dekalog* is based on the Ten Commandments (also known as the Decalogue), as presented in Exodus 20 and Deuteronomy 5. All ten films are set in the same Warsaw housing development, and all deal with one or more of the commands God handed down to Moses, as recorded in the Bible.

The films are not moral fables. The connections between the stories and the corresponding commandments are not always explicit. Dekalog 1 ("You shall have no other gods before me") concerns a father and son who put their faith in science and computers to determine the safety of the ice of nearby ponds for

22 Fury

Fury, *a 2014 film directed by David Ayer,* chronicles the events of a five-man crew of a Sherman tank named Fury in Nazi Germany during the last days of World War II. One of the five men—Boyd "Bible" Swan (Shia LaBeouf)—gets his nickname for quoting Bible verses during this dangerous mission. He tells one of the other men, "Here's a Bible verse I think about sometimes. Many times. It goes: And I heard the voice of the Lord saying: Whom shall I send and who will go for us? And . . . I said: Here am I, send me!" (compare to Isaiah 6:8).[2]

One of the other men mumbles, "Send me," and their sergeant, Don "Wardaddy" Collier (Brad Pitt), immediately adds its location in the Bible: "Book of Isaiah, Chapter six."[3] In Isaiah 6 the verse alludes to God's call to Isaiah to go and prophesy to the people.

Boyd also tries to convert other soldiers and quotes Bible verses over fallen comrades, praying the Lord's Prayer (Matthew 6:9–13) as they take their last breaths. Boyd and Wardaddy share Bible verses and philosophize about things like what Jesus might think of Hitler. Wardaddy asks, "Boyd, you think Jesus loves Hitler?"[4] Boyd answers matter-of-factly, "I'd assume so. If Hitler accepted Jesus into his heart and got baptized, he'd be saved." But realizing it may be too late for Hitler, Boyd adds, "Ain't gonna save him from Man's justice."[5] ■

skating. Dekalog 5 ("You shall not murder") explores the motivations of a lawyer defending a teenager who is guilty of a senseless murder. Dekalog 10 ("You shall not covet . . . anything that is your neighbor's") deals with two brothers who become obsessed with their late father's stamp collection.

Dekalog raises provocative questions concerning the rules of morality that govern society but offers few easy answers. ■

Above Right: Mirosław Baka (center) in the film *Dekalog* (1989).

23

The Shawshank Redemption

Based on a Stephen King novella, The Shawshank *Redemption* is often cited as one of the most popular movies ever made. The plot concerns Andy Dufresne, a wrongly accused man trying to adjust to life inside a maximum-security prison. The most dangerous threat to his well-being is the cold and calculating Warden Norton, whose venal, psychotic nature is (barely) veiled by a veneer of piousness and holier-than-thou platitudes.

In a key scene in the film, the warden and his guards conduct a surprise inspection of Andy's cell. Unknown to Andy, the warden wants to use Andy's accounting skills for a money-laundering scheme. Unknown to the warden, a poster on Andy's wall hides a tunnel he's digging to freedom.

The two antagonists eye one another briefly. When the warden notices the Bible Andy is holding, he asks what Andy's favorite passage is.

"Watch ye therefore: for ye know not when the master of the house cometh," Andy replies, using Jesus's words in Mark 13:35 (KJV) to slyly reference the warden's unannounced visit.

The warden tells Andy that he prefers John 8:12: "I am the light of the world: he that followeth me shall not walk in darkness, but shall have the light of life" (KJV).

The warden hands back Andy's Bible and says, "Salvation lies within."[6] At the conclusion of the film, after Andy has escaped and blown the whistle on Norton's criminal enterprise, those words come back to haunt the warden. He opens the front flap of Andy's Bible and finds an inscription, written by Andy, that says, "Dear Warden. You were right. Salvation lay within."[7]

He opens it further to find that the pages inside have been cut out in the shape of a rock hammer. Andy had used his Bible as a hiding place for the tool he used to dig his escape tunnel. ∎

Tim Robbins and Morgan Freeman in the film *The Shawshank Redemption* (1994).

24

The Truman Show

The Truman Show is a prescient fable that anticipates the rise of reality television. The story centers on Truman Burbank, a man who doesn't realize that every aspect of his life is staged reality, filled with actors playing the roles of his family, friends, neighbors, coworkers, and acquaintances. Overseen from on high (in a control room located far above the enormous soundstage that serves as Truman's universe) by its God-like creator-director Christof, *The Truman Show* is broadcast daily to millions of viewers worldwide. The film uses biblical imagery to establish the relationship between Christof and his human "creation."

In an interview, Christof presents the bucolic island community he has created for Truman as an Eden of sorts, a place where

Truman is safe and cared for. Yet Truman begins to question his existence and test the biblical concepts of free will and preordination as he ponders what lies beyond the island he's never left. When he tries to escape his destiny by sailing away, similar to Jonah's sailing to Tarshish instead of Nineveh, as God had asked (Jonah 1), Christof manufactures a storm to turn him around. When that doesn't work, he speaks to Truman from on high, in a manner reminiscent of God speaking to Moses as written in Exodus.

Christof's tender speech to Truman, in which he reminisces about the day of Truman's birth, echoes the words of Jeremiah 1:5: "Before I formed you in the womb I knew you." ∎

Above Right: *The Truman Show*, advance movie poster (1998).
Jim Carrey in the film *The Truman Show* (1998).

25 The Children of Men

The Children of Men, *based loosely on P. D. James's novel of the same name,* offers a chilling look at the apparent end of the human race. According to the film's director, Alfonso Cuarón, the title is a Catholic allegory derived from Psalm 90:3: "Thou turnest man to destruction; and sayest, Return, ye children of men" (KJV).

The story is set in 2027. Worldwide infertility has created an extinction-level threat. No new babies have been born—anywhere on the planet—for eighteen years.

Britain's totalitarian government has its hands full deporting all immigrants and suppressing rebel uprisings. Theo Faron, a man with government connections, is recruited by a rebel group called The Fishes to secure transit papers for a young immigrant woman named Kee. Theo is able to get the papers, but only under the condition that he accompany Kee.

While on the run after a deadly ambush, Theo discovers that Kee is keeping a secret with worldwide implications: she's pregnant. He agrees to help her rendezvous offshore with a ship (portentously named *Tomorrow*) that belongs to the Human Project, scientists who are working to restore human fertility.

To get there, Theo and Kee have to infiltrate a heavily guarded immigrant camp. As soon as they get inside the camp, however, Kee goes into labor and gives birth to a baby girl. Rebel forces, with their own agenda for Kee's baby, storm the camp and kidnap Kee and her daughter.

The movie culminates with a brutal firefight between government forces and the rebels, who are holed up in an abandoned apartment building. Theo manages to rescue Kee and the child. Unable to hide the baby any longer, the three make their way out of the apartment building as the rebel fighters and immigrant occupants look on in wonder. The fighting stops as the combatants gaze at the only hope for the future of humankind.

The notion of the birth of a baby bringing peace and offering hope in a time of darkness is an obvious allusion to the Advent narrative recorded in Luke 2—and especially the words often taken as prophecy found in Isaiah 9:6. ■

Above and Left: Movie stills from the film *The Children of Men* (2006).

26 Macbeth
William Shakespeare

The works of William Shakespeare share literary and linguistic roots with the Geneva Bible, which was first published in 1560, around the time of Shakespeare's birth. The cadences and rhythm of language in Shakespeare's works and the Geneva Bible are remarkably similar. The fact that Shakespeare was familiar with the Bible is evident in each of his plays. Scholars have found more than 1,200 references and allusions to the Bible in Shakespeare's works.

A case in point is his masterwork *Macbeth*.

In act 1, scene 7, Macbeth acknowledges his similarities to Judas Iscariot by paraphrasing Jesus's words to his traitorous disciple in John 13:27: "That thou doest, do quickly" (KJV).

In act 2, scene 3, Macduff refers to Duncan's body as "the Lord's anointed temple," echoing the assertion in 1 Corinthians 3:16 that human beings are temples of God. Macduff's emphasis on the fact that Duncan was "the Lord's anointed" ruler emphasizes the monstrous nature of Macbeth's crime.

In act 4, scene 2, Lady Macduff's complaint regarding her husband's absence—"All is the fear and nothing is the love"—is a reference to 1 John 4:18: "There is no fear in love."

These examples are merely the tip of the iceberg. More than fifty references to the Bible can be found in *Macbeth*. Shakespeare's writing is deepened by its biblical allusions. Likewise, seeing (or hearing) the Bible in a Shakespearean context can give new shading to a familiar passage. ∎

Above: The title page of *Macbeth*, printed in the Second Folio (1632), Folger Library Digital Image Collection.

Left: Illustration from *Macbeth* in *The Works of William Shakespeare*.

A COMPLETE
COMMENTARY,
WITH
Etymological, Explanatory, Critical
and Classical NOTES
ON
MILTON's Paradise Loft:
EXPLAINING

1. All the Hebrew, Chaldaic, Arabic, Syriac, Phœnician, Egyptian, Greek, Latin, Italian, Spanish, Portuguese, Danish, Ruffian, Tatarian, Saxon, Teutonic (or German) Dutch, Norman, (or Old French) Old English (or Scottish) Indian, American and Miltonian Words, i. e. Thofe of the Author's own Coining, thro' the whole Poem.

2. All the difficult Terms of Divinity, Philofophy, Mathematics, Aftronomy, Aftrology, Hiftery, Geography, Architecture, Navigation, Anatomy, Surgery, Chymiftry, Alchemy, Hunting, Hawking, Gardening, and other Human Arts and Sciences.

3. All the fine Epithets, the Mythology (or Fables) of the Antients) all the Figures of Grammar and Rhetoric, Comparifons, Similies, Digreffions, different Perfons; and fetting all the Tranfpofed Sentences in a plain English Profe Order; with many new Theological, Critical, Hiftorical and Political Obfervations, never publifhed before. For without fuch a Work the Poem is ufelefs to moft Readers of it.

In magnis voluiffe fat eft.   Tibull.

By JAMES PATERSON, M.A.

27 Paradise Lost

John Milton

John Milton's narrative poem Paradise Lost, which spans twelve books, is an epic retelling of the fall of humanity. Milton's reason for pouring more than five years of his life into creating his magnum opus was equally epic. According to book 1, his aim was to "justify the ways of God to men."

The poem's origins are found in Genesis 3, but Milton does not confine himself to the biblical account of Eden and its loss. Milton also builds a complex narrative in which a defeated Satan does the following:

- Contemplates his next move with his followers in hell
- Learns of a new universe that God has created
- Leaves hell and makes his way through Chaos
- Flies to the sun and tricks an angel named Uriel into showing him where God's human creation lives
- Gets caught in—and banished from—the garden of Eden
- Returns as a serpent
- Tempts Eve to eat the fruit of the forbidden tree
- Gets condemned to hell in the form of a serpent

A second narrative arc, involving Adam and Eve, also includes extrabiblical plot developments. According to Milton, God sends the angel Raphael to the garden to warn Adam and Eve about Satan. Raphael tells them humanity was created to replace the fallen angels in heaven. After Adam and Eve give in to the serpent's temptation, God sends the angel Michael to reveal the future consequences of their sin.

Though their narratives differ radically, both Milton's poem and the Genesis account end with Adam and Eve's expulsion from the garden of Eden. ■

Top: Antique copy of *A Complete Commentary on Milton's Paradise Lost* by James Paterson.

28

A Christmas Carol

Charles Dickens

Few authors can boast a stable of characters as artfully named as those of Charles Dickens. Martin Chuzzlewit, Wackford Squeers, and Uriah Heep are just a few of his memorable literary inventions. Perhaps the most famous character he ever created, however, can trace his name to the pages of the Hebrew Bible.

In 1 Samuel 7, the Israelites are under attack from the Philistines. Desperate, they beg the prophet-priest Samuel to pray for them in their upcoming battle. Samuel not only prays but also offers a sacrifice to God, who responds by giving victory to the Israelites.

Samuel commemorates God's intervention by erecting a stone. He "called its name Ebenezer; for he said, 'Till now the LORD has helped us' " (1 Samuel 7:12). The name *Ebenezer* means "stone of help."

In *A Christmas Carol*, references to God, the Bible, and God's intervention in the affairs of humanity abound. Tiny Tim, the afflicted son of Scrooge's clerk, Bob Cratchit, tells his father on their way home from church that he hoped people saw him with his crutch so as "to remember on Christmas Day who made lame beggars walk and blind men see."

The miser Ebenezer Scrooge is visited on Christmas Eve by these characters:

- The Ghost of Christmas Past, who reminds him of the love and joy he once knew
- The Ghost of Christmas Present, who opens his eyes to the needs of others
- The Ghost of Christmas Yet to Come, who shows him what happens to those who are driven by greed and selfishness

Unlike the portrayal in the movies, in the book, Scrooge's experience with the ghosts takes place over three successive nights. On the third day, Scrooge experiences new life, representative of the Bible's description of Jesus being resurrected on the third day. As Christmas morning dawns, Scrooge is a changed man. ∎

Left: Charles Dickens (1812–1870) in his study at Gad's Hill Place.
Above: Charles Dickens (1812–1870), portrait from the 1860s.

29 Uncle Tom's Cabin
Harriet Beecher Stowe

There is a story, most likely folk legend, that when President Abraham Lincoln met Harriet Beecher Stowe at the start of the Civil War, he remarked, "So this is the little lady who started this great war." Such was the impact of Stowe's antislavery novel. Yet credit for the reactions to *Uncle Tom's Cabin* also must be shared with the book that looms large in the novel: the Bible.

The Bible is quoted or alluded to more than one hundred times in Stowe's story. Uncle Tom, the character around whom the story revolves, refuses to allow the horrors of slavery to dim his Christian faith. At one point, his evil owner resolves to crush Tom's belief in God, but he cannot. Tom continues to read the Bible ("his Bible seemed to him all of this life that remained"). Tom holds fast to his Christian faith even as he is beaten to death.

Tom's noble character and steadfast faith inspire not just his fellow slaves but also his murderous overseers and even his former master, who, after learning of Tom's death, frees all his slaves. ■

Top: *Uncle Tom's Cabin*, historic site.
Right: 1800s carte-de-visite (CDV) of Harriet Beecher Stowe (1811–1896), abolitionist and author of *Uncle Tom's Cabin*.

30 The Old Man and the Sea
Ernest Hemingway

In his masterful tale of one man's battle with a giant marlin, Ernest Hemingway makes liberal use of crucifixion imagery to draw parallels between Santiago (the old man) and Jesus. Hemingway describes the sacrifice inherent in Santiago's mission and links it to the supreme sacrifice of Jesus, who, according to Christian teaching based on the Bible, gave his life to save humanity.

The scene in which Santiago struggles to haul his mast up a hill after his fishing excursion alludes to the Bible's depiction of Jesus's struggle carrying his cross to Golgotha for his crucifixion.

When Santiago's fishing line slices the palms of his hands, his bloody wounds unmistakably mirror the wounds the Bible describes on Jesus's hands at his crucifixion. Hemingway emphasizes the point later in the story when sharks arrive to devour the carcass of the marlin.

Eventually Santiago makes it home and collapses on his bed with his face down, his arms extended, and his palms up, in a classic crucifixion pose.

Like Jesus, Santiago finds gain in apparent loss, victory in apparent defeat, and life in apparent death. ■

Top: Spencer Tracy in the film *The Old Man and the Sea* (1958), based on Ernest Hemingway's book

31 Catch-22
Joseph Heller

Joseph Heller uses the Bible as a touchstone in his anti-war masterpiece, *Catch-22*. Though the references are fleeting, they lend gravity to his descriptions of the absurdities of war and add pathos to the plight of his characters.

Heller's description of a crewman named Kraft, who "had lived innocuously for a little while and then had gone down in flame over Ferrara on the seventh day, while God was resting,"[8] paints a bleak existential picture of casualty. According to Genesis 2, God rested from his work after six days of creation.

When Major Major's sergeant learns that the soldier he trained now outranks him, his reaction is to brood "for hours in his tent like Saul, receiving no visitors."[9] Saul, the first king of Israel, is described in the Hebrew Bible as brooding because he likely suffered from depression. The sergeant in *Catch-22* broods because Major Major's promotion means he's no longer allowed to "beat hell out of any man in his outfit."[10]

Elsewhere Heller alludes to the parting of the Red Sea to convey the ease with which the intimidating Major de Coverley (whose identity is so mysterious that his first name is never used) makes his way through a crowd of officers. The fact that several other characters in the book do Major de Coverley's bidding without being asked suggests a godlike quality to his character. ■

Above: The novel *Catch-22* by Joseph Heller (1961).
Right: Alan Arkin in the film *Catch-22* (1970).

32

The African Queen

The African Queen *marks the only screen pairing* of Hollywood icons Humphrey Bogart and Katharine Hepburn. Bogart plays Charlie Allnut, the seedy-looking captain of the *African Queen*, a supply boat. Hepburn plays Rose Sayer, a prim and proper British Methodist missionary in East Africa. Rose's brother (and fellow missionary) is apparently familiar with the Bible, alluding to Song of Solomon 1:5 in describing his sister: "Not comely among the maidens, but she, too, can be a servant in the house of the Lord. Even for such as she, God has a goodly purpose."

At the outbreak of World War I, German forces kill Rose's brother and burn down their village. Charlie rescues her in the *African Queen* and tries to convince her to sit out the war with him in their backwater location. Rose has other ideas. When she learns the boat is hauling blasting gelatin and cylinders of oxygen and hydrogen, she convinces Charlie to rig the boat as a giant torpedo. Together they will navigate treacherous waters to destroy the large German warship that patrols the lake at the river's end.

The biblical theme of sacrifice—more specifically, of sacrificial love—drives the narrative. The suicidal nature of the mission reveals the sacrificial spirit of Charlie and Rose. Along the way, these two mismatched souls fall in love. As they near their destination, the boat hits a stretch of reedy shallows. Charlie jumps into the water to pull it through the muck.

When he climbs back on the boat, Rose screams. He is covered with leeches. She pours salt on his skin to remove them while Charlie shudders in revulsion. All too soon, though, Charlie realizes he must go back into the water. In a profound display of sacrificial love, Rose joins him. Together they pull the *African Queen* through—and eventually fulfill their mission. ∎

Above: Katharine Hepburn with Humphrey Bogart in the film *he African Queen* (1951).
Top: T*he African Queen* original movie poster (1951).

33 The Robe

The 1950s were Hollywood's golden age for biblical epics. Preceding both *Ben-Hur* and *The Ten Commandments*, director Henry Koster's *The Robe* is built on one of the more unusual premises for a Bible story. Richard Burton stars as Marcellus Gallio, the young Roman tribune who won Jesus's robe in a dice game during the crucifixion. Victor Mature stars as Demetrius, Marcellus's Christian servant.

Profoundly affected by the crucifixion of Jesus, Marcellus can't bring himself to touch Jesus's robe. So Demetrius takes it and departs. The Roman emperor Tiberius, fearful of the burgeoning Christian movement, orders Marcellus to destroy the robe and assemble a list of Jesus's followers. However, when Marcellus tracks down Demetrius and his Christian community, he is touched by the robe and healed of his mental anguish. Marcellus becomes a Christian.

Marcellus accompanies Demetrius and the apostle Peter on a missionary trip to Rome. The new emperor, Caligula, orders Marcellus to stand trial for being an enemy of Rome and then sentences him to death. The movie ends with Marcellus and Diana, the love of his life who has also become a Christian, walking to their martyrdom together.

By surrounding the main (fictional) characters with actual biblical and historical figures, *The Robe* achieves a sense of authenticity that many lesser epics lack. Viewers are left with a depiction of the extreme challenges that the earliest Christians may have experienced. ∎

Top: Jean Simmons and Richard Burton in the film *The Robe* (1953).

34

On the Waterfront

Many movies feature characters who portray what are thought of as messianic qualities. However, few of these cinematic messianic archetypes are female. *On the Waterfront* is perhaps the best-known example of a movie that bucks the trend.

In Elia Kazan's masterpiece, Eva Marie Saint plays Edie, an innocent young woman who has been raised by Catholic nuns far from the brutality and corruption of the New York docks where her father and brother work. When Edie returns home, however, she chooses to sacrifice her purity and enter the fallen world of dockworkers in order to help save them.

The docks are run by the mob-connected union leader, Johnny Friendly, who decides which union guys will get work on a given day and which ones won't. Friendly and his henchman terrorize the dockworkers, skimming money from union coffers, demanding a percentage of laborers' pay, and silencing those who threaten to expose their corruption.

When Edie's brother and another worker are killed for cooperating with the Waterfront Crime Commission, the local priest, who is crusading to end corruption on the docks, calls their deaths "crucifixions" because they died to help others. Whoever stands by idly as this happens, the priest continues, "shares the guilt of it just as much as the Roman soldier who pierced the flesh of our Lord to see if he was dead."[11] The priest then concludes his impassioned speech with a plea that closely paraphrases Matthew 25:40: "If you do it to the least of mine, you do it to me!"[12]

Eventually, the mantle of suffering Savior falls on Terry Malloy, a lackey of Friendly's, who finds the courage to stand up to the union boss despite the consequences. Director Kazan uses a bloody wound on Terry's hand, reminiscent of the wounds the Bible describes on the crucified Jesus, to make clear his intentions.

The movie ends with the savagely beaten Terry stumbling to his worksite, while his followers and enemies look on to break the power of "evil" on the docks. ∎

Left: Marlon Brando and Karl Malden in the film *On the Waterfront* (1954).
Above: Marlon Brando in *On the Waterfront* (1954).

35 Guys and Dolls

The setting of this rollicking musical is the Save a Soul inner city mission, run by Sister Sarah Brown. Sister Sarah catches the attention of Sky Masterson, a high-rolling gambler with a reputation for betting big on just about anything. Sky pursues Sarah through a predictable array of romantic setbacks, misunderstandings, and changes of heart. He and his fellow gamblers save the mission in the end by attending a service and confessing their sins.

The Bible is alluded to and quoted directly throughout the film, usually in a humorous or ironic context. In one scene, after Sky is slapped by Sarah, he mentions Matthew 5:39. "Don't bother looking it up," he tells her, "it's the bit about turning the other cheek."[13]

In another scene, Sky points out an error on a Bible-verse-of-the-day card that attributes the quote "No peace unto the wicked" to the Bible's book of Proverbs. This quote comes from Isaiah 57:21. Sarah is incredulous at Sky's knowledge of the Bible. "I imagine there's only one thing that's been in as many different hotel rooms as I have: the Gideon Bible," he explains. "Don't tangle with me on the Good Book. I must've read it through at least a dozen times."[14] ∎

Right: Guys and Dolls original movie poster (1955).

36
The Seventh Seal

The title of director Ingmar Bergman's masterpiece is drawn from Revelation 8:1: "When the Lamb opened the seventh seal, there was silence in heaven for about half an hour." The silence of God is the primary theme of *The Seventh Seal*.

The film is set in a fourteenth-century Swedish village. A knight named Block, returning home from the Crusades with his squire Jöns, finds that his homeland is being devastated by the plague. Block encounters Death, in the (much-imitated) form of a white-faced human figure wearing a black cowl. Block challenges Death to a chess match, believing that if he wins, he can prolong his life.

Meanwhile, others in the village struggle to come to grips with their impending deaths in light of their religious faith. They question God's existence in the face of such misery and suffering. Block, too, struggles with difficult questions. "Why must God hide in vague promises and invisible miracles?"[15] he asks Death, whom he mistakes for a priest at one point.

Alas, no answers are forthcoming. After losing the chess match, Block invites a group of people back to his castle, where he assumes they will be safe from the plague. Yet Death follows them and claims everyone in the castle. The movie ends with the group being led over a hill while they perform a macabre dance of death.

And all the while God remains silent. ■

Top: Bengt Ekerot and Gunnar Björnstrand in the film *The Seventh Seal* (1957).

Left: Filming of *The Seventh Seal* at Filmstaden (1957).

37 Barabbas

Like **The Robe,** *which preceded it by eight years,* *Barabbas* anchors its fictional story in a biblical setting. Anthony Quinn plays Barabbas, the notorious criminal who, according to the Bible, was chosen to be set free instead of Jesus as part of a Jewish Passover tradition. In the Bible, after Jesus is led away to his crucifixion, the newly freed Barabbas exits the Gospel narrative.

Richard Fleischer's 1961 epic imagines Barabbas's life following his release. In the film, Barabbas returns to his old life, only to find that Rachel, the woman he loves, has become a follower of the man who was crucified in Barabbas's place. Barabbas witnesses not just Jesus's crucifixion but also his empty tomb three days later. He visits Jesus's disciples to see if they have taken his body. Like Rachel, they believe Jesus has risen from the grave.

When Rachel is stoned to death for preaching about Jesus, Barabbas returns to his life of crime. He is arrested and sent to work in sulfur mines. From there, he becomes a gladiator and eventually wins his freedom.

The burning of Rome proves to be a pivotal moment for Barabbas. Believing that Christians were responsible for starting the blaze, he shows his allegiance by setting fire to several buildings. He is arrested yet again and imprisoned with other Christians, including the apostle Peter, who converts him to a true faith in Jesus. The movie ends with the mass crucifixion of Barabbas and his fellow Christians. ■

Top: Anthony Quinn in the film *Barabbas* (1961).

38 Lilies of the Field

Lilies of the Field, the title of director Ralph Nelson's beloved film, comes from Jesus's words as recorded in Matthew 6:28–29: "Consider the lilies of the field, how they grow: they neither toil nor spin, yet I tell you, even Solomon in all his glory was not arrayed like one of these."

Homer Smith (played memorably by Sidney Poitier in an Academy Award–winning role) is a traveling handyman who encounters a group of Eastern European nuns trying in vain to do small repairs on a farm in the Arizona desert. Homer assists them by fixing their roof.

He tries to persuade the Mother Superior to pay him for his efforts by quoting Luke 10:7: "The labourer is worthy of his hire" (KJV). She counters by quoting Matthew 6:28. Thus begins the relationship between the handyman and the nuns, who, Homer learns, have fled their Communist homeland to start a mission on the inhospitable Arizona property that was willed to their order.

The nuns see Homer as the answer to their prayers—the man who will help them build a chapel for the impoverished people of their town. Homer tries to resist—and continues to try to get paid by quoting Bible verses to the Mother Superior—but in the end, he comes to grips with the fact that he is the man for the job. ■

Left: Sidney Poitier in the film *Lilies of the Field* (1963).

39 The Bible: In the Beginning . . .

The Bible: In the Beginning . . . differs from other biblical film epics in its omnibus approach to the source material. In its three-hour running time, the film covers several stories from the first twenty-two chapters of Genesis.

As the title implies, the movie opens with the story of creation. Breathtaking images of nature convey the newness and wonder of the events described in Genesis 1.

The segment, featuring Adam and Eve, plays up the childlike qualities of the first humans and emphasizes the devastating consequences of the Fall.

The complicated, tragic, and ultimately violent relationship between Cain and his brother Abel is explored in the third section of the film.

A short segment on the tower of Babel focuses on the egotism and pride of Nimrod, the king who oversees the construction of the tower and must bear the consequences of that construction.

The segment featuring Noah (played by the film's director, John Huston) takes a lighthearted approach to the ark's construction and the task of collecting the animals.

The movie concludes with the story of Abraham and Sarah and their struggle to come to grips with God's promise to give them a son. Screen icon George C. Scott digs deeply into his role as the patriarch of the Jewish people. Particularly wrenching is the scene in which Abraham is faced with the prospect of sacrificing the son he has so desperately longed for.

The Bible: In the Beginning . . . was intended as the first of several films that would tell the complete story of the Hebrew Bible. Though the reviews and box office were generally good for this initial outing, no sequel was ever made. ∎

Top: Noah's ark in the film *The Bible: In the Beginning . . .* (1966).

40 A Man for All Seasons

The historical drama A Man for All Seasons, based on Robert Bolt's stage play of the same name, won six Academy Awards, including Best Picture and Best Actor (Paul Scofield). It is ranked forty-three on the British Film Institute's list of the greatest British films of all time.

The title character is Sir Thomas More, the sixteenth-century Lord Chancellor of England, who drew the ire of King Henry VIII by refusing to accommodate the king's divorce and remarriage—and later by refusing to sign an oath acknowledging the king as the head of the Church of England.

More draws on the Bible—often in sly references—to underscore the moral weight of his position. In one scene, a cardinal who is an ally of the king tries to excuse the monarch's infidelity by pointing out that his bride-to-be is fertile, unlike the queen. "Catherine's his wife and she's barren as a brick; are you going to pray for a miracle?"[16]

"There are precedents,"[17] More replies.

More eventually pays a dear price for clinging to his biblical principles. He is arrested for treason and imprisoned in the Tower of London. At his trial, he refuses to speak so that his accusers will have no testimony to use against him. Instead, they convict him on the perjured testimony of one of his acquaintances. More is executed for holding fast to his belief in the Bible. ∎

Above: Robert Shaw as Henry VIII and Paul Scofield as Sir Thomas Moore in the film *A Man for All Seasons* (1966).

41 Cool Hand Luke

The film **Cool Hand Luke** reveals its biblical influence not just in its dialogue and plot but also in its shot composition. Paul Newman's character, Luke Jackson, is a World War II veteran who is sentenced to two years on a Florida chain gang for destroying parking meters during a night of drunken revelry. He is also one of a long line of messianic figures in the pantheon of great American films.

Some film critics believe Luke's prison uniform number (37) is an allusion to a verse in the book of the Bible that bears his name—Luke 1:37, which says, "Nothing will be impossible with God." This is a fitting verse for the movie's Luke and his seemingly impossible antics.

Luke makes a name for himself among his fellow prisoners—and in a sense converts them to be his "disciples"—by defying authority and refusing to conform to expectations.

The movie frames key scenes in such a way to drive home the parallels between Luke and Jesus. In one such scene, after winning a bet by eating fifty hard-boiled eggs, an exhausted and nauseated Luke collapses on top of a table, with his arms outstretched and one foot over the other in a classic crucifixion pose. A lingering overhead shot leaves little doubt as to director Stuart Rosenberg's intentions.

Similarly, the last shot of the movie superimposes a photo of Luke, who has been killed by the prison boss, over a scene of his fellow inmates working alongside a road. As the camera pulls back into a panoramic vista, the overhead perspective reveals two roads intersecting, framed to resemble a cross. ∎

Above Left: Paul Newman and George Kennedy in the film *Cool Hand Luke* (1967).
Right: Paul Newman as Luke Jackson in the film *Cool Hand Luke* (1967).

42

The Pilgrim's Progress

John Bunyan

John Bunyan's masterpiece, whose full title is *The Pilgrim's Progress from This World to That Which Is to Come; Delivered under the Similitude of a Dream*, is widely regarded as a landmark of English literature and the pinnacle of Christian allegory. The first part of the narrative follows the everyman Christian as he makes his way from the City of Destruction to the Celestial City. Along the path, he is befriended and beset by a host of allegorical characters. His journey represents the challenges faced by faithful pilgrims trying to make their way through this world with their faith intact. The second part of the narrative follows Christian's wife, Christiana, and their four sons as they make the same journey.

Bunyan fills his allegory with so many references to the Bible that listing them all would be an encyclopedic endeavor. Here are a few of the most obvious:

- The great burden that weighs Christian down, the knowledge of his sin, comes from the book in his hand. That book is the Bible.
- On his journey, Christian stops before Mount Sinai, the place where God gave Moses the Ten

Commandments, according to the books of Exodus and Deuteronomy.

- As Christian crosses the frightening Valley of the Shadow of Death, he hears the words of Psalm 23 being spoken and takes comfort from them.
- Christian refers to Lady Wanton as Potiphar's wife, the woman who tried to entice Joseph in Genesis 39.
- The city of Vanity Fair is described with a quote from Ecclesiastes 11:8: "All that cometh is vanity" (KJV).
- "Remember Lot's wife" refers to the story of the destruction of Sodom and Gomorrah recorded in Genesis 19. ∎

Left: *Christian Reading in His Book* by William Blake (1757–1827).
Above: Title page of the first edition of *The Pilgrim's Progress* (1678) by John Bunyan (1628–1688).

43 Jesus Christ Superstar

Jesus Christ Superstar, the film version of Andrew Lloyd Webber's controversial stage musical of the same name, seems to follow the Gospel narrative of Jesus's adult life. Disciples commit themselves to him. Crowds gather to hear him teach. Jewish leaders plot against him. Jesus is given a hero's welcome when he arrives in Jerusalem. He drives greedy merchants from the temple. He shares a final meal with his disciples. He prays in a garden. Judas betrays him. Jesus is arrested, put on trial, and beaten. His disciple Peter denies knowing him. Judas commits suicide. Jesus is crucified.

A closer examination, however, reveals why many Christians consider the film (and the musical on which it is based) blasphemous. For one thing, Judas serves as Jesus's voice of conscience. He accuses Jesus of getting caught up in his own fame. He sings about stripping away the myths about Jesus so that people can see he is just a man. He encourages Jesus to focus more on helping the poor and less on enjoying the trappings of his fame.

In the end, Jesus comes off as a well-meaning but ultimately misguided man whose popularity led to circumstances beyond his control—and who, in the end, saw a martyr's death as his best hope for lasting fame. The film narrative ends with Jesus's crucifixion; no mention is made of the resurrection. ∎

Top: Ted Neeley as Jesus in the film *Jesus Christ Superstar* (1973).

44 The Hiding Place

Based on Holocaust survivor Corrie ten Boom's autobiography of the same name, *The Hiding Place* tells the true story of the ten Boom family—Corrie, her sister Betsie, and their father, Casper—who shelter Jews in their home during the Nazi invasion of Holland. Casper, a devoted reader of the Bible, welcomes the opportunity to assist "God's chosen people."

When a Dutch collaborator blows the whistle on them, the family is arrested. Casper dies before his sentence can be carried out. Corrie and Betsie eventually are sent to Ravensbruck concentration camp.

Inside Ravensbruck, Betsie encourages Corrie to hold fast to their shared Christian faith. They hold forbidden worship services in the camp, using a Bible they manage to smuggle in. The sisters quote passages to comfort and give hope to each other and their fellow prisoners.

Betsie dies of illness in the camp, but Corrie is released in December 1944 through what is later revealed to be a clerical error. All her fellow prisoners were sent to the gas chamber a month after Corrie's release.

Corrie ten Boom used her experiences as the basis for a Christian ministry that continued until her death in 1983. The title of her autobiography and the accompanying film is drawn from David's words in Psalm 119:114: "You are my hiding place and my shield; I hope in your word." ∎

Top: Julie Harris as Betsie ten Boom and Jeannette Clift as
Corrie ten Boom in the film *The Hiding Place* (1975).

45 The Old Dark House

The Old Dark House *reunites James Whale and Boris Karloff,* the director and star (respectively) of *Frankenstein*, for one of the earliest entries in the "spooky house" subgenre of horror films. As a violent thunderstorm rages, five travelers are forced to take shelter for the night in the mansion of the eccentric Femm family. As the night progresses, the travelers discover just how dangerously eccentric the Femms are.

Horace Femm is prone to hysteria. His sister Rebecca is a religious fanatic. Their decrepit 102-year-old father lives in an upstairs bedroom. Their brother Saul seems to be the only normal person in the house. However, Saul's friendly demeanor masks homicidal insanity.

He believes that he is possessed by the spirit of King Saul—of Hebrew Bible fame. Furthermore, he believes that one of the guests, Roger Penderel, is possessed by the spirit of David, Saul's enemy and rival.

As he attempts to kill Roger, the movie's Saul paraphrases 1 Samuel 18:9–11: "But Saul was afraid of David because the Lord was with him and was departed from Saul. And it came to pass on the morrow that the evil spirit came upon Saul and he prophesied in the midst of the house. And David played upon the harp with his hand. And there was a javelin in Saul's hand."[18]

Though Roger is wounded by Saul, all five travelers manage to survive the night. When the storm ends at dawn, they flee as quickly as possible—while Horace cheerfully bids them farewell, as though nothing had happened. ■

Above: Scene from the film *The Old Dark Horse* (1932).

46 Chariots of Fire

Above: *Chariots of Fire* original movie poster (1981).
Below: Ian Charleson as Eric Liddell in the film
Chariots of Fire (1981).

The Bible's fourth commandment—"Remember the Sabbath day, to keep it holy" (Exodus 20:8)—figures prominently in *Chariots of Fire*, the story of two runners who represented Great Britain in the 1924 Olympics. Harold Abrahams is a Jewish university student who must overcome anti-Semitism to achieve his goal of winning a gold medal. Eric Liddell is a devout Christian who runs to glorify God.

Liddell is devastated to learn that the Olympic heat for his specialty race, the one hundred meters, will be held on a Sunday. His Christian faith will not allow him to dishonor what some call the "Christian Sabbath," even for the Olympics. On the day his heat is run, Liddell is found in his Scottish church, delivering a sermon from Isaiah 40 that includes the following passage: "But they who wait for the LORD shall renew their strength; they shall mount up with wings like eagles; they shall run and not be weary; they shall walk and not faint." Abrahams, meanwhile, wins the gold medal in the event.

Moved by Liddell's principled stand, a teammate generously gives his place in the 400-meter race (which is run on a Thursday) to Liddell, who improbably (yet predictably, in a cinematic sense) wins the gold. The British team returns home as Olympic champions and moral exemplars. ■

47 Raiders of the Lost Ark

The lost object of the title of this film is the ark of the covenant, perhaps the holiest of all relics. According to Exodus 25, the ark was a chest made of acacia wood and overlaid with gold. Built to God's precise specifications, it housed the stone tablets that contained the Ten Commandments, a pot of manna, and Aaron's rod.

More significant than the chest itself or its contents, however, was the ark's cover, also known as the "mercy seat," which featured the figures of two cherubim. According to the book of Exodus, God spoke to Moses from between the two cherubim.

Priests carried the ark ahead of the Israelites as they made their way from Mount Sinai to the land of Canaan. The Israelites credited their victory over Jericho and other Canaanite cities to God's power, which emanated from his presence with the ark.

The ark was lost to history when the Babylonians destroyed Jerusalem around 586 BC. In *Raiders of the Lost Ark*, a George Lucas–Steven Spielberg blockbuster film, set in 1936, a Nazi archaeological expedition is on the verge of uncovering the ark, which could give Hitler the power to conquer the world. Only the intrepid archaeologist-adventurer Indiana Jones can prevent the ark from falling into Nazi hands.

Not only do the Nazis gain possession of the ark, but they also manage to capture Jones and his love interest, Marion. At the film's climax, the two watch helplessly as the Nazis open the ark. It's then that God's power is revealed. Spirits emerge to kill the entire contingent of Nazis.

According to the Hebrew Bible, anyone who touched the ark or looked inside would die (1 Samuel 6:19; 2 Samuel 6:6–7).

Only Indiana Jones and Marion, who closed their eyes to protect themselves, survive. God had told Moses, "You cannot see my face, for man shall not see me and live" (Exodus 33:20). ∎

Right: Mayan art.   Top: Harrison Ford in the film *Raiders of the Lost Ark* (1981).

48 Amadeus

Miloš Forman's film Amadeus, based on the play of the same name by Peter Shaffer, explores the rivalry between Antonio Salieri, the court composer for the eighteenth-century Holy Roman Emperor Josef II, and Wolfgang Mozart, one of the most celebrated musical prodigies the world has ever known.

Salieri thinks of himself as a servant of God whose musical successes are God's gifts for his piety. His opinion changes when he meets the young genius Mozart.

Salieri recognizes the divine gift in Mozart yet struggles to understand why God would choose to speak through such an unworthy vessel. In his crisis of faith, Salieri comes to believe that God is using Mozart to mock Salieri's own mediocre musical talents.

Some compare the relationship between Salieri and Mozart to the rivalry between Cain and Abel in the book of Genesis. Cain resented his brother Abel because God accepted Abel's sacrifice and not his. Cain took revenge by murdering Abel in a field (Genesis 4:8). Salieri is also consumed by a vicious jealousy of Mozart and plots his failure and demise. He tricks Mozart into writing a requiem mass, promising him an enormous sum of money, but plans to pass it off as his own work and then murder Mozart.

However, unlike the Cain and Abel account, Salieri's murderous plan is thwarted when Mozart dies before finishing the requiem. Salieri is convinced that God chose to kill Mozart rather than allow Salieri to have any of the glory. The bitter, nearly insane composer resigns himself to his fate as the patron saint of mediocrity.

When a priest attempts to comfort him with the words "All men are equal in God's eyes,"[19] a principle found in Romans 2:11, Salieri mocks him with a simple question: "*Are* they?"[20] ∎

Above: Tom Hulce as Mozart in the film *Amadeus* (1984).

49

The Mission

The Mission, a sober tale of eighteenth-century missionaries ministering in the jungles of Argentina and Paraguay, features a stunning sequence that illustrates the Bible's teachings concerning penance and atonement. Father Gabriel (Jeremy Irons), a Spanish Jesuit priest, is there to build a mission and convert the Guaraní people to Christianity. Rodrigo Mendoza (Robert De Niro) is a slave trader whose guilt sends him back to the village of the very people he kidnapped and sold into slavery. He is on a quest for absolution for his sin. As part of his penance, he makes a treacherous climb, dragging behind him a heavy bundle containing his armor and sword.

When Mendoza reaches the top of a cliff, he comes face to face with the Guaraní people, who recognize him as the evil man who preyed upon them. The Guaraní approach Mendoza with their knives drawn—and demonstrate their forgiveness by cutting away the rope that attaches Mendoza to his bundle and throwing the heavy burden off the cliff.

The Guaraní become a symbol in this film of God's forgiveness and atonement (Romans 8:1–2).

Moved by the Guaraní's acceptance, Mendoza expresses his desire to help at the mission, and Father Gabriel gives him a Bible. ■

Top: Jeremy Irons as a Spanish Jesuit who goes into the wilderness in the film *The Mission* (1986).
Above: Robert De Niro as a slave trader in the film *The Mission* (1986).

50 Bruce Almighty

In Bruce Almighty, *Jim Carrey stars as Bruce Nolan,* a local TV news reporter in Buffalo, New York, who gets passed over for a coveted anchor's position and then loses his job. He blames God for his troubles and suggests that the Almighty is the one who should be fired. Shortly thereafter, Bruce receives a visit from God, in the form of Morgan Freeman. God offers Bruce all his powers and the opportunity to do God's job better than he does for a week.

Biblical allusions are sprinkled throughout the film. For example, the address of God's company is 77256 23rd Street. The numerical equivalent of dialing PSALM on a phone pad is 77256. So God's address is Psalm 23. And Bruce's prayer e-mail service is Yahweh.com—a reference to the Bible's name for God, Yahweh.

Predictable hilarity ensues as Bruce uses his newfound powers for his own benefit and amusement. He teaches his dog to use a toilet. He transforms his old junker into a high-performance supercar. He humiliates his rival during a live broadcast.

Yet Bruce's stint as God is grounded by two biblical touchstones: prayer and free will. He is overwhelmed by the sheer number of prayer requests he receives every day (in the form of voices in his head). When he answers yes to all of them, he throws the city of Buffalo into chaos.

Likewise, Bruce—as God—finds that he cannot force people to love him or to make certain decisions. He must honor their freedom to make their own choices, including those of his long-suffering girlfriend who leaves him when his power starts to go to his head.

In the end, a sadder-but-wiser Bruce asks God to relieve him of his powers and then places himself at God's mercy. God responds by reuniting Bruce with his girlfriend in a most unusual—and painful—way. ∎

Above: Morgan Freeman in the film *Bruce Almighty* (2003).

Above: Morgan Freeman and Jim Carrey in the film *Bruce Almighty* (2003).

51 Beowulf
Anonymous

The epic poem Beowulf *recounts the battle* between the warrior Beowulf and the demon-monster Grendel, who lives in a swamp and terrorizes the Danish king Hrothgar and his men. Set in pagan times, the poem references a variety of ancient superstitions. Yet it also contains an odd sprinkling of biblical allusions—some of which are intertwined with pagan myths to create a peculiar hybrid.

Consider this allusion to the Bible's book of Genesis in a description of Grendel: "He spawned in that slime, conceived by a pair of those monsters born of Cain, murderous creatures banished by God, punished forever for the crime of Abel's death."

Hrothgar's men are pagans who "sacrificed to the old stone gods," in violation of the first commandment of Exodus, which says, "You shall have no other gods before me" (20:3). These men know "neither God nor His passing as He walks through our world, the Lord of heaven and earth; their ears could not hear His praise or know His glory."

The poem's author despairs their pagan nature: "Oh, cursed is he who in times of trouble has to thrust his soul in the fire's embrace, forfeiting help; he has nowhere to turn. But blessed is he who after death can approach the Lord and find friendship in the Father's embrace."

Throughout the poem, as the author describes Beowulf's courage and skill in battle, he is careful to give credit to the God who created and empowered him. Consider the scene in which Beowulf finally prevails over Grendel: "The monster wrenched and wrestled with him but Beowulf was mindful of his mighty strength, the wondrous gifts God had showered on him: He relied for help on the Lord of All, on His care and favor. So he overcame the foe, brought down the hell-brute." ∎

Top Right: Viking warrior photographed by Fernando Cortes.
Right: The first folio of the poem *Beowulf*, written primarily in the West Saxon dialect of Old English.

52 Jane Eyre
Charlotte Brontë

Jane Eyre *is the story of a young orphan girl.* Sharp-eyed readers will spot more than a dozen references to the Bible in Charlotte Brontë's debut novel.

In an imaginary conversation with her spiteful Aunt Sarah, Jane admits she should forgive her aunt. Jane says, "For you knew not what you did"—an unmistakable reference to Jesus's words on the cross in Luke 23:34.

Mr. Brocklehurst, the mean-spirited minister who runs a charity institution for orphan girls, accuses Jane of being deceitful by paraphrasing Revelation 21:8: "All liars will have their position in the lake burning with fire and brimstone."

As she is about to marry Rochester, the moody owner of the estate where she works as a governess, Jane learns that he has a mentally unstable wife he keeps locked away. Jane compares the resulting death of her hopes to the tenth plague of Egypt, as described in Exodus 11, the death of all firstborn children.

Rochester refers to his home, Thornfield Hall, as "this accursed place—this tent of Achan." The allusion concerns Achan, a character in the Hebrew Bible who stole accursed things from Jericho after the Israelites' victory there and hid them in his tent. Achan's disobedience brought God's judgment on the entire nation.

When Jane accepts a position as a schoolmistress from clergyman St. John Rivers, he cautions her not to look back, using Lot's wife as a cautionary tale. In Genesis 19:26, while fleeing the doomed cities of Sodom and Gomorrah, Lot's wife couldn't resist stealing one last glance at what she was leaving behind—despite the fact that an angel had instructed her not to. Because of her disobedience, she turned into a pillar of salt.

Jane returns to Thornfield Hall, only to find that the estate has been burned down and Rochester is living in seclusion. His wild appearance reminds her of King Nebuchadnezzar, who is described in Daniel 4 as living as a feral creature and whose hair and nails subsequently grow to resemble eagles' feathers and bird claws.

The two lovers are reunited. After Rochester loses his sight, he compares the comfort he receives from Jane to the comfort King Saul received from David's harp playing, as described in 1 Samuel 16.

Jane, referring to the intimacy of her marriage to Rochester, describes herself as "bone of his bone, flesh of his flesh," using Adam's exclamation upon Eve's creation in Genesis 2:23.

At the end of the novel, Jane refers to a letter she receives from St. John Rivers, who has become a missionary to India. She describes him as anticipating "his incorruptible crown," a reference to the reward that awaits believers, according to 1 Corinthians 9:25.

The final sentence of the novel, delivered by St. John Rivers, mirrors the final words of the Bible in Revelation 22:20–21: "Daily [God] announces more distinctly, 'Surely I come quickly!' and hourly I more eagerly respond,—'Amen; even so come, Lord Jesus!'" ■

Right: Mia Wasikowska as Jane in the film *Jane Eyre* (2011).

53 Les Misérables
Victor Hugo

The tension between two key biblical themes—mercy and justice—lies at the heart of Victor Hugo's masterpiece, *Les Misérables*. Jean Valjean is finally released from prison after serving a nineteen-year sentence for stealing a loaf of bread to feed his sister's starving children. Police inspector Javert informs Valjean that he is not really free; he will always be guilty of his crime.

Valjean's criminal record prevents him from finding honest work. In desperation, he steals silver from a church bishop, who had graciously welcomed the freed convict into his home, consistent with the words he had written in the margin of a Bible: "The door of a physician should never be closed; the door of a priest should always be open." When Valjean is caught with the loot, the bishop saves him from going back to prison by claiming that he gave the silver to Valjean. The bishop's stunning act of mercy transforms Valjean. For the first time in a long time, he sees himself as a man worthy of compassion. He destroys his old identity papers—which violates the conditions of his parole—and uses the silver to become an honest businessman.

Javert then begins a single-minded ambition to put Valjean back in prison. For years he pursues his adversary—not out of hatred but of an unbending sense of justice. Ultimately his obsession with justice causes Javert to take his own life.

The characters of Javert and Valjean together represent the prophet Micah's words: "And what does the LORD require of you but to do justice, and to love kindness, and to walk humbly with your God?" (Micah 6:8). ∎

Top: National flag of the French Republic (France), photographed by Alexey V. Smirnov. Left: Original illustration by Émile Bayard (1837–1891) for *Les Misérables* (1862) by Victor Hugo. Caption reads: "Cosette sweeping."

 **54** The Grapes of Wrath

John Steinbeck

In **The Grapes of Wrath,** a tale of the hardworking Joad family trying to survive the horrors of life in Oklahoma during the Dust Bowl, author John Steinbeck sets up an unmistakable parallel between the Joads' plight and that of the ancient Hebrews in Egypt. The Joads' trip to California becomes an exodus—a quest to save themselves and start anew.

Tom Joad, the oldest son and symbol of Moses, is a reluctant but determined leader. When he kills a man along the way, his actions are reminiscent of Moses's killing of an Egyptian in Exodus 2:12.

The Joads and the Hebrews both cross a body of water—the Colorado River and the Red Sea, respectively—before they begin the desert portion of their journeys. As they near California, the Joads begin to hear rumors from other travelers that their destination is not the paradise that they imagine. Likewise, the spies that entered Canaan attempted to dissuade the Hebrews from taking possession of the land by telling tales of giants who lived there.

The Joads are forced to endure nightmarish, overcrowded migrant camps and border guards who try to send them back to Oklahoma. The Hebrews are forced to battle for their land against the formidable Edomites, Moabites, and Ammonites.

Even the title of the novel alludes to the Bible, comparing the struggles of the Joads to the horrors of the end times: "So the angel swung his sickle across the earth and gathered the grape harvest of the earth and threw it into the great winepress of the wrath of God" (Revelation 14:19). ∎

Above Right: *The Grapes of Wrath* (1939) by John Steinbeck (1902–1968).
Top: Henry Fonda (right) in the film *The Grapes of Wrath* (1940).

55 Brideshead Revisited
Evelyn Waugh

Brideshead Revisited: The Sacred & Profane Memories of Captain Charles Ryder has been called an apologia for Catholicism. Author Evelyn Waugh described the book as his attempt to explain his Roman Catholic faith. The biblical concepts of grace and conversion play key roles throughout the narrative.

Charles Ryder is a college student in 1923 when he meets Sebastian Flyte, the son of a British lord. Sebastian invites Charles to his home, Brideshead Castle, where Charles meets Sebastian's family. His mother, Lady Marchmain, along with his older brother, Lord Brideshead, and his youngest sister, Cordelia, are all devout Catholics. His father, Lord Marchmain, is an Anglican who converted to Catholicism in order to marry.

Sebastian and his younger sister, Julia, are somewhat less devout.

Charles, who has given little thought to religion, is taken aback by the family's Catholicism. As the years pass and the relationships between Charles and various members of the Flyte family shift, the spiritual views of various characters change.

The novel ends with Charles, now a soldier, returning to a deserted Brideshead Castle, which has been conscripted for military use. He wanders into the private chapel, which had been closed since the death of Lady Marchmain but reopened to accommodate worshiping soldiers. He kneels and offers a prayer, implying his own conversion to Catholicism. ∎

Top: Castle Howard in North Yorkshire, England, has appeared as Brideshead in both the 1981 television serial and 2008 film adaptation of Evelyn Waugh's novel *Brideshead Revisited*.

56 The Stand
Stephen King

The premise of The Stand could not be more biblical. Stephen King's postapocalyptic epic deals with the final showdown between good and evil. After a bioengineered virus wipes out 99.4% of the earth's population, survivors find themselves drawn to one of two camps. The forces of good, led by 108-year-old Mother Abigail, are mysteriously drawn to Boulder, Colorado, where they attempt to reestablish a democratic society.

The forces of wickedness, led by a figure named Randall Flagg—essentially the embodiment of evil—are drawn to Las Vegas, where they submit to Flagg's tyrannical rule. Flagg and his forces amass a cache of weapons, including a nuclear bomb, and make plans to launch an assault on Boulder.

Mother Abigail, in turn, sends a small group of her most trusted followers on a secret mission to confront Flagg in Las Vegas. When the surviving members of the group are captured and marked for public execution, the stage is set for the novel's stunning climax.

References to God, his work, and his judgment are scattered throughout the novel, as are comparisons between Mother Abigail and Moses and Jesus. When she suspects that her pride has hindered her ability to lead, Abigail heads to the wilderness alone, as did Moses, as recorded in the book of Exodus, and Jesus, according to Matthew 4.

The book's most obvious reference to the God of the Bible, however, is found in the climactic scene on the Las Vegas Strip. As Flagg conjures a supernatural ball of energy to silence someone in the crowd, the ball is suddenly transformed into a hand—an image that is familiar to readers of Daniel 5—that triggers the bomb, killing all of Flagg's followers. ∎

Above: Apocalyptic city ruins, illustration by Victor Zastol'skiy.

57 The Song of Bernadette

Based on the popular novel of the same name, *The Song of Bernadette* tells the story of a young woman's nineteenth-century encounters with one of the most beloved characters of the New Testament. Set in Lourdes, France, in 1858, the film follows Bernadette Soubirous, a Catholic schoolgirl from an impoverished family who creates a scandal in her village when she reports seeing visions of a "beautiful lady"—a lady the townspeople believe to be Mary, the mother of Jesus.

The lady appears to Bernadette in a small grotto near the city dump. She instructs Bernadette to return to the spot every day for the next fifteen days, promising to appear to her each of those days. During one appearance, the lady instructs Bernadette to drink and wash from a spring—a spring that Bernadette cannot see. Bernadette digs a hole until water begins to flow—water that seems to have healing properties. The scene calls to mind passages in the Exodus account in which God provides water for the Hebrew people in the wilderness. It also aligns with the words of Psalm 74:15: "You split open springs and brooks."

News of Bernadette's visions travels quickly. Some people celebrate her blessing; others question her sanity. When the situation threatens to get out of hand, the grotto is closed. The local Catholic authority refuses to conduct an official investigation.

When the emperor's son falls ill, however, the child's nanny sneaks into the grotto to retrieve water from the spring for him. The child recovers, and the emperor declares the grotto reopened.

Bernadette becomes a nun and faces emotional abuse from Sister Vauzous, her former schoolteacher, who is now one of the instructors in the convent. Vauzous eventually confides to Bernadette that she is jealous that God would choose such an unworthy girl to receive his visions when Vauzous herself had suffered so much in his service.

Bernadette, who is dying of tuberculosis, despairs that she will never see the lady of her visions again. On her deathbed, however, the Blessed Mother appears to her one last time, much to Bernadette's delight. ∎

Right: Scene from the film *The Song of Bernadette* (1943).

58 It's a Wonderful Life

The words of Hebrews 13:2, "Do not neglect to show hospitality to strangers, for thereby some have entertained angels unawares," set the scene for *It's a Wonderful Life*, a holiday classic.

George Bailey is facing a dark night of the soul. Through no fault of his own, he finds himself in dire financial straits. His company, Bailey Building and Loan, is facing a shortfall of eight thousand dollars on Christmas Eve—the day his brother Harry, who's been awarded the Medal of Honor for saving an entire transport of troops during World War II, is scheduled to come home. It's also the day a bank examiner arrives to audit Bailey Building and Loan's books.

Through flashbacks we discover that George's life has been one of thwarted dreams and selfless sacrifice. For the citizens of Bedford Falls, the Building and Loan is a lifeline—the only alternative to the other financier in town, the evil banker/slumlord, Mr. Potter.

With nowhere else to go, George turns to Potter for a loan, offering his life insurance policy as collateral. Potter sneers at his request and points out that George is worth more dead than alive.

George tries to drown his misery at a local bar, to no avail. After muttering a desperate prayer, he drives away, crashes his car, and then trudges through the snow to a local bridge, where he contemplates suicide. Before he can jump, however, he sees someone fall into the water. George dives in to save the man, who turns out to be his guardian angel, Clarence—the answer to George's prayer.

When George suggests that things would be better if he had never been born, as did the biblical character Job facing his trauma, Clarence shows him just how wrong he is. Together the two men head back to town—a place where George Bailey never existed—and discover a much darker and gloomier landscape. They interact with George's friends and family, who are markedly different people. George is given the rare opportunity to witness the difference his life made in the lives of others.

With this new, life-changing perspective, George returns home to find his family and friends—and one of the happiest endings in movie history—waiting for him. ■

Top: Donna Reed and James Stewart in the film *It's a Wonderful Life* (1946).

59 Diary of a Country Priest

Diary of a Country Priest, *by acclaimed French director* Robert Bresson, is widely acknowledged as a landmark in world cinema. Along with *The Passion of Joan of Arc*, it has been called one of the greatest movies venerating the Catholic faith ever made.

Bresson's bleak masterpiece concerns a young priest who struggles to find acceptance in his parish in the village of Ambricourt, France. He eats very little—bread, wine, and a little potato soup—due to a stomach ailment that leaves him weak and often nearly helpless.

His parishioners and colleagues gossip about him and make fun of his ascetic lifestyle. The young priest responds in a manner that is similar to Jesus in the Bible by refusing to dignify their allegations with a response or defend himself against their accusations (Matthew 25:13–14). Instead, he continues to minister in the face of indifference and hostility, teaching Bible classes and helping those in need.

Eventually he is diagnosed with stomach cancer and faces the existential question of why he should minister and try to bring hope to people when death is unavoidable. The priest comes to grips with his mortality—and his inability to find grace in a cruel world—in the home of a colleague who has renounced his former calling and chosen a life outside of God's service. ∎

Top: Claude Laydu and Martine Lemaire in the film *Diary of a Country Priest* (1951).

60 Babette's Feast

In the film **Babette's Feast,** set in a remote village on the western coast of Denmark in the nineteenth century, two elderly sisters oversee the Protestant ministry started by their late father. The sisters, who decades earlier sacrificed their own chances for happiness and marriage for the sake of their father, preside over an aging, insular congregation whose Christian faith has curdled into piety and strictness.

Their lives are upended by the arrival of Babette, a young French woman recommended to the sisters as a housemaid by one of their former suitors. The sisters cannot afford to pay her, so Babette offers to work for free in exchange for room and board.

For the next fourteen years, Babette cooks for the sisters and their congregation, slowly replacing the bland food they associate with piety and self-sacrifice with a tastier fare. The villagers are unaware that Babette is the former head chef of a renowned Parisian restaurant and that, through a friend, she plays a lottery every year.

Babette wins ten thousand francs in the lottery, but instead of returning to her former life, she decides to spend it all on one unforgettable meal for the congregation. She orders exotic ingredients, the likes of which the villagers have never tasted, and sets about preparing a sumptuous seven-course meal.

The congregation, afraid of falling into the sin of sensual pleasure, agrees to eat the meal but determines not to show any enjoyment of it whatsoever. Still, Babette's selfless gift overwhelms them. The mystical power of her culinary skills transforms them. A genuine sense of forgiveness, peace, and love settles over them as they dine together. A visiting military officer, who has the culinary acumen to appreciate the meal's brilliance, paraphrases Psalm 85:10 in a toast of gratitude: "Mercy and truth have met together. Righteousness and bliss shall kiss one another."[21] ∎

Above Right: *Babette's Feast* original movie poster (1987).
Above Left: Stéphane Audran (center) as Babette in the film *Babette's Feast* (1987).

61 Leap of Faith

Steve Martin stars as Jonas Nightengale, a con artist posing as a Christian faith healer in *Leap of Faith*. When his tour bus breaks down in the farming community of Rustwater, Kansas, Nightengale decides to make the best of the situation by holding a few tent revival meetings. Though the locals have been hit hard by drought, Nightengale, along with his entourage, plan to con them out of what money they have left using fake healings and freewill offerings.

During his stay, Nightengale makes the acquaintance of several people in town, including Marva, a waitress in the local café, and her brother Boyd, who lost the use of his legs following a car accident. Marva suggests that Boyd's paraplegia may be psychosomatic.

Nightengale manages to gain the trust of the towns-people with a few manufactured miracles. Despite being a huckster and a con artist, during his services he accurately quotes several Bible verses, including Ephesians 6:10–11. When Boyd, who has come to believe that Nightengale can heal him, walks during one of his healing services, Nightengale suspects that Boyd is a con artist too.

After the service, the angry Nightengale returns to the empty tent and reveals his true colors by mocking Christianity and the crucifix that serves as the centerpiece of his stage. Outside, though, he sees people who have been truly impacted by what they witnessed.

Moved by their faith, Nightengale quietly packs his bags and slips away. He hitches a ride with a trucker. As they drive away, a torrential down-pour begins, signaling the end of the drought. Nightengale realizes he's witnessing genuine divine intervention. The movie ends with Nightengale hanging out the truck window, praising Jesus for the rain. ∎

Top Right: Steve Martin as Jonas Nightengale in the film *Leap of Faith* (1992).
Left: Steven Martin as a Christian con artist in the film *Leap of Faith* (1992).

62 A River Runs Through It

Based on Norman Maclean's autobiographical account of growing up in Montana with a father and brother who shared his passion for fly fishing, *A River Runs Through It* is filled with allusions to the Bible. Set in the 1920s, the movie tells the story of Presbyterian minister John Maclean and his two sons: Norman, steady and dependable, and Paul, mercurial and reckless. The resemblance to the characters in Jesus's parable of the prodigal son is intentional. The film also suggests shades of Cain and Abel in the relationship between Norman and Paul, as Norman wrestles with the question of whether he is his doomed brother's keeper.

Reverend Maclean imbues in his sons a deep appreciation for the sanctity and healing potential of time spent hip-deep in the Blackfoot River casting for trout. He refers to his fishing pole as a rod, in reference to Psalm 23:4: "Your rod and your staff, they comfort me." He reminds his sons that Jesus's disciples were fishermen and leads them to assume that the favorite among them, John, was a dry-fly fisherman.

On what turns out to be the trio's last fishing excursion together, Reverend Maclean spends time reading his Bible on the shore and then shares with Norman an insight that has occurred to him. Referring to the first few verses of the Gospel of John, Maclean reminds his son that the "word" preceded creation and then points out that if you listen closely, you can hear the words under the water. ∎

Right: Brad Pitt, Craig Sheffer, and Tom Skerritt in the film
A River Runs Through It (1992).
Top: Craig Sheffer, Brad Pitt, and Tom Skerritt in the film
A River Runs Through It (1992).

63 Rudy

This much-beloved sports movie tells the inspiring tale of Daniel Eugene "Rudy" Ruettiger, who has dreamed of attending Notre Dame and playing for the Fighting Irish football team from the time he was a little boy. Unfortunately, his lack of size, skills, and academic standing makes his dream a long-shot bid at best.

Yet Rudy will not be denied. He works hard at a local community college, desperately trying to earn the grades he needs to be accepted into Notre Dame before his junior year, when it will be too late. With time running out and things looking bleak, Rudy turns to a sympathetic priest to ask why God hasn't answered his prayers.

Echoing the words of Psalm 27:14 ("Wait for the Lord; be strong, and let your heart take courage; wait for the Lord!"), the priest reminds Rudy that God answers prayers in his own time.

Rudy presses, asking if there's something the priest can do for him, implying that the priest might have some pull with the Almighty. The priest informs him that in thirty-five years of religious training, he has discovered only two hard, incontrovertible facts: "There is a God, and I'm not him."[22] ■

Top: Sean Astin in the film *Rudy* (1993).

64 Beloved
Toni Morrison

Toni Morrison's book *Beloved* (1987) won a 1988 Pulitzer Price for Fiction and was made into a movie of the same name starring Oprah Winfrey. The novel, set in the context of slavery's toll on self-worth and relationships, contains a wide range of biblical themes. Examples include the story of Lot's wife (Genesis 19:15–26); a discussion of how pride leads to all sorts of human problems (Proverbs 16:18); the story of Jesus feeding the multitudes (Matthew 14:13–21; Mark 6:31–44; Luke 9:10–17; John 6:5–15); and the four horsemen of the Apocalypse (Revelation 6:1–8).

Morrison quotes Romans 9:25 from the King James translation in her epigraph: "I will call them my people, which were not my people; and her beloved, which was not beloved." The apostle Paul used these words from the biblical book of Hosea (2:23) in his letter to the Romans (9:25–26) to describe God's love for all people. It is possible that this verse provided the inspiration for not only the title of Morrison's book but also the themes of love and acceptance within the book. ■

Danny Glover and Oprah Winfrey in the film *Beloved* (1998).

65 The Apostle

The Apostle, a film written and directed by Robert Duvall, stands apart from most similarly themed Hollywood movies in its complex portrayal of a Christian evangelist. Texas Pentecostal preacher Sonny Dewey isn't a charlatan or a con man. He isn't jaded or cynical about his faith. He genuinely believes what he preaches.

When he comes upon an accident scene, his first instinct is to try to get the gravely injured driver to place his faith in Jesus before he dies. Sonny truly cares about the well-being of the souls in his congregation. His one-sided conversations with God are loud, raucous, questioning, and sincere. He preaches from the Bible as one who understands its truths but wrestles with their implications.

Sonny is also a deeply flawed man. When he learns that his wife is having an affair with the church's youth pastor—and that she plans to divorce him and take his congregation—he snaps. At a Little League baseball game, Sonny attacks the youth pastor with a bat and then flees the state. The youth pastor later dies from his injuries.

Sonny ends up in the bayous of Louisiana, where he changes his name and takes over a small, predominantly African American congregation from its retired pastor. Using a radio ministry on a local station, Sonny increases the attendance—and the spiritual fervor—at the church.

His life on the run comes to an end when his wife recognizes his voice on the radio and alerts authorities. Police officers arrive at the church to arrest Sonny during an evening service but allow him to finish one last heartfelt sermon before they take him away. ■

Top Right: Robert Duvall as Sonny Dewey in the film *The Apostle* (1997).
Left: Robert Duvall as a Pentecostal preacher in the film *The Apostle* (1997).

# 66 Pleasantville

In this comic fantasy film, David and Jennifer, siblings from the 1990s, are teleported via their TV remote control into a 1950s sitcom called *Pleasantville* (a show modeled on the likes of *Leave It to Beaver* and *The Adventures of Ozzie and Harriet*). While laughs are mined from the introduction of 1990s mores and attitudes into the squeaky-clean environment of 1950s sitcom suburbia, director Gary Ross's movie aims for something deeper.

Some moviegoers believe the black-and-white world of Pleasantville represents the garden of Eden. The suburban community is an unspoiled refuge, a place where sin and nonconformity don't exist. The sexually precocious Jennifer initially assumes the role of the serpent. She seduces her boyfriend, an act that introduces free will and

"the knowledge of good and evil" (Genesis 2:17) into the paradise of Pleasantville.

As in the Genesis narrative, the results are immediate and profound. The "innocence" of Pleasantville is disrupted. Having tasted the proverbial forbidden fruit, the denizens of Pleasantville have their eyes opened and their perspectives broadened.

This awakening is cleverly represented in the film by colorization. Those who succumb to the temptation of a new way of thinking or who experience passion are filled in with color, much to the astonishment, disgust, and horror of their staunchly black-and-white families, friends, and acquaintances. ■

Top: Joan Allen and Tobey Maguire in the film *Pleasantville* (1998).

67 Saving Private Ryan

In **Saving Private Ryan,** Steven Spielberg's harrowing account of D-Day and one ill-fated mission that followed, a squad of eight American soldiers are ordered to locate and extricate Private Ryan from the battlefields of Normandy. Ryan's three brothers were killed in action within days of one another, and the War Department wants to ensure that their mother does not lose all four of her sons in combat.

The film is replete with religious overtones, opening and closing with row upon row of crosses and Stars of David marking soldiers' graves in a French cemetery. Several scenes show dying soldiers clutching their crosses or rosaries.

The squad that the War Department sends out to look for Private Ryan includes a deadly, efficient sniper, Private Jackson, who is presented as a devout Christian.

Jackson prays before missions, insists that God made him "a fine instrument of warfare,"[23] and, most memorably, quotes passages from the book of Psalms before he fires his weapon.

While targeting German machine gunners on Omaha Beach, he chooses Psalm 22:19: "But be not thou far from me, O LORD: O my strength, haste thee to help me" (KJV). In the final battle scene, Jackson takes refuge in a church tower, hinting that he is in a position of godly authority over his Nazi targets. He quotes Psalm 144:1–2: "Blessed be the LORD my strength which teacheth my hands to war, and my fingers to fight: My goodness, and my fortress; my high tower, and my deliverer; my shield, and he in whom I trust; who subdueth my people under me" (KJV). ∎

Above: Tom Hanks in the film *Saving Private Ryan* (1998)

68 The Matrix

The Matrix *presents a dystopian future* in which nothing is as it seems. Sentient machines have enslaved most of humanity in order to produce energy from their body heat. Humans are unaware of their enslavement because they are wired into a simulated reality known as the Matrix. They believe they have freedom because the Matrix convinces them they do. In actuality, they are inert slaves.

Compare that setup to Jesus's words on slavery to sin recorded in John 8:31–45. Jesus emphasizes that *his* truth sets people free. First it opens their eyes to their slavery; then it shows them the way out.

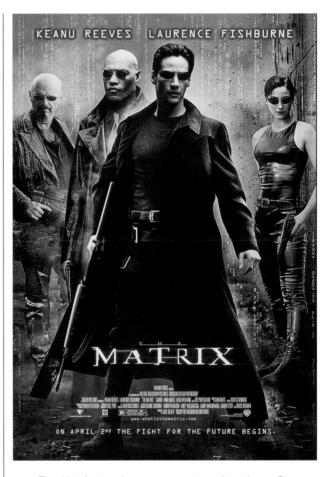

The Matrix, too, has a presenter of truth—a Chosen One charged with leading a rebellion against the machines. His name is Neo. As with Jesus in the Bible, Neo's coming is said to be foretold by prophets. In *The Matrix* and its two sequels, Neo battles to fulfill his mission to bring salvation and freedom to the human race.

The Matrix mirrors many New Testament themes such as messiahship, betrayal by a disciple, crucifixion, resurrection, and the sending of the Holy Spirit. The film also features such Bible names as Thomas and Zion, and even a clear allusion to a Bible verse (Mark 3:11) in the the words "Mark III No. 11" inscribed on the ship *Nebuchadnezzar*. ■

Above Left: Carrie-Anne Moss in the film *The Matrix* (1999).
Above Right: *The Matrix* original movie poster (1999).

69 Mission: Impossible

In the first outing of the enormously successful **Mission: Impossible** ***franchise,*** Tom Cruise's agent, Ethan Hunt, works to uncover the identity of the mole who framed him for the botched assignment that led to the deaths of his entire Impossible Missions Force team. The only information he has to go on is that the mole is working with an arms dealer named Max on something called "Job 314."

Hunt figures out that Job 314 is actually a reference to a Bible verse—Job 3:14 ("with kings and counselors of the earth who rebuilt ruins for themselves"). The mole's code name is Job.

Eventually Hunt discovers that the mole is his traitorous boss, Jim Phelps, who faked his own death during the botched assignment. The clue that trips up Phelps is a Bible he stole from a Chicago hotel room. ■

Tom Cruise in the film *Mission: Impossible* (1996).

The Nativity Story *combines the Advent accounts* found in the Gospels of Matthew and Luke to portray the events surrounding the birth of Jesus. While the movie remains fairly true to the Bible narrative, it also challenges audiences to consider aspects of the story not recorded.

For example, Mary is portrayed as a girl who still enjoys playing with other children in her hometown of Nazareth. She is far from excited about her arranged betrothal to Joseph. She doesn't love the man; in fact, she barely knows him.

Her pregnancy scandalizes the town and devastates Joseph. Her parents suspect that she was raped by a Roman soldier and warn her that she could be put to death for violating her betrothal vows. When Joseph takes her back (following a visit from an angel), he, too, is shunned by "polite" society.

The scheming of the evil King Herod, the difficult journey to Bethlehem, the gift-giving mission of the magi, the shepherds' encounter with the angels, and the baby in the manger are all stories found in the Bible that are given a fresh perspective in this reverent film by director Catherine Hardwicke. ■

Above: Joseph and Mary journeying to Bethlehem in the film *The Nativity* Story (2006).

71 World Trade Center

This harrowing dramatization of the events of 9/11 includes the story of former United States Marine sergeant Dave Karnes, who witnessed the World Trade Center attacks on television at his accounting office in Connecticut. In the movie, Karnes drives to a local church, where he prays with the pastor that God will lead him to survivors trapped in the rubble of the Twin Towers.

Sergeant John McLoughlin and Officer Will Jimeno, two Port Authority first responders trapped in the service elevator shaft of the North Tower, do some praying of their own. At one point, as debris rains down on them, McLoughlin screams the Lord's Prayer from Matthew 6:9–13.

The movie presents Karnes as the answer to the men's prayers. Dressed in his Marine Corps uniform, Karnes makes his way past the barricades to Ground Zero, where he hears a noise coming from the service elevator shaft. McLoughlin and Jimeno are saved, thanks to Sergeant Karnes's prayer-guided mission. ■

Top: Scene from the film *World Trade Center* (2006).
Above: The World Trade Center behind the Statue of Liberty, photographed by Joseph Sohm.

72 The Story of Ruth

One of the lesser-known biblical epics of the 1950s and 1960s is an adaptation of the book of Ruth. Shot in CinemaScope by director Henry Koster, the film depicts the young Ruth as a devout worshiper of the Moabite god Chemosh. So great is her dedication to Chemosh that she helps prepare another Moabite girl, Tebah, to be sacrificed to the pagan god.

A Judean artisan named Mahlon, who has been instructed to polish a crown for Tebah, asks some pointed questions of Ruth, causing her to question the existence of Chemosh. Ruth and Mahlon fall in love and embrace Jewish monotheism together, a decision that doesn't sit well with the pagan powers that be in Moab. Mahlon is sentenced to work in a quarry for the rest of his life. His life proves to be regrettably short—he dies after an escape attempt.

It is at this point in the film that the biblical narrative begins. Ruth agrees to accompany her mother-in-law, Naomi, to Naomi's homeland of Israel. There she meets and marries Boaz, a kinsman of Naomi. The film ends quoting the final words of the biblical book of Ruth. ■

Above: Tom Tryon and Elana Eden in the film *The Story of Ruth* (1960).
Top Right: Scene from the film *The Story of Ruth* (1960).

73 The Book of Eli

In this postapocalyptic thriller directed by Albert and Allen Hughes, the Book of Eli is a Bible—the only Bible left in the world in the year 2043. War has decimated the planet. Believing that the Bible was the cause of the war, people burned every other copy.

Denzel Washington plays Eli, a man who, for thirty years, has been making his way west in the aftermath of the apocalypse. He believes the Bible holds the key to the future of humanity and is determined to deliver it to Alcatraz Island, where certain artifacts are being gathered in preparation to begin civilization again.

Along the way he encounters murderous marauders and assorted evildoers, including one, Carnegie, who shoots Eli in the stomach and takes his Bible, which is covered by a locked flap. Carnegie believes the Bible unlocks the key to leadership. When he manages to unfasten the flap, he discovers it is written in braille. Eli is blind. Only Carnegie's love interest can read it, and she refuses.

Eli, meanwhile, makes his way to Alcatraz, where he recites the Bible from memory while another man writes it down, word for word. Shortly after he helps transcribe the entire Bible, Eli dies of his gunshot wound. ■

Top: Mila Kunis and Denzel Washington in the film *The Book of Eli* (2010).
Above Right: Gary Oldman in the film *The Book of Eli* (2010).

 Exodus: Gods and Kings

Exodus: Gods and Kings *(2014)* is *The Ten Commandments* (1956) of the twenty-first century, with Ridley Scott replacing Cecil B. DeMille in the director's chair and Christian Bale filling Charlton Heston's sandals as Moses.

Like *The Ten Commandments*, the movie *Exodus: God and Kings* takes a fair amount of dramatic license with the biblical story of Moses, the Hebrew child raised as Egyptian royalty who leads the Hebrew people out of slavery in Egypt, through the wilderness of Sinai, and to the land of Canaan.

Here are some of the scenes that are not found in the Bible:

- Moses and his Egyptian half brother Rameses ride into battle together against the Hittites, and Moses saves Rameses's life. Later, Rameses, the new pharaoh, forces Moses to admit his true identity by threatening to cut off the arm of Moses's Hebrew sister, Miriam.
- In exile, Moses gets caught in a rockslide on a mountain. Submerged in mud and suffering from a broken leg, he is visited by God in the form of a child.
- Back in Egypt, Moses trains Hebrew slaves in combat so they can battle against Pharaoh's forces. The plague of water turning to blood is caused by a group of crocodiles attacking a boat of fishermen.

The movie ends with the Hebrew people en route to the land of Canaan, with the Red Sea behind them and the Ten Commandments in their possession. Moses, now an elderly man, sees the childlike representation of God walking among the Hebrew people. ∎

Above: Christian Bale as Moses in the film *Exodus: Gods and Kings* (2014).

Noah *uses the events of Genesis as mere tie-ins* for its scenes. They are incorporated when they align with the story and discarded when they don't. The result is a movie that entertained moviegoers and critics, for the most part, but frustrated many Bible purists.

After experiencing visions warning of a coming flood, Noah (played by Russell Crowe) takes his family to visit his grandfather Methuselah. Along the way, they stumble onto the scene of a massacre that left as its only survivor a girl named Ila. Rather than leave her to fend for herself, Noah adopts her. The killers, followers of Tubal-Cain (a descendant of the Bible's first murderer, Cain), chase Noah and his family into the dark region of the Watchers, fallen angels who have been turned to stone golems for helping humans after the Fall.

From there, the action comes fast and furious. Methuselah gives Noah a seed from the garden of Eden that immediately brings forth a network of streams and an entire forest. Noah uses the wood from the forest to build the ark. Tubal-Cain and his followers attempt to seize the ark but are driven back by the Watchers.

With an eye toward the future of the human race, Noah goes to a nearby camp to find wives for his three sons. He sees humans being traded and slaughtered for food and becomes convinced that the Creator wants the human race to end.

Animals follow the newly forged streams to the ark, where Noah puts them into a deep sleep with a special

incense. Noah's oldest son, Shem, takes Ila for his wife. His middle son, Ham, finds a woman for himself as the rain begins to fall, but he must leave her behind when she gets caught in an animal trap.

Tubal-Cain sneaks onto the ark as the floodwaters rise. Onboard, Noah discovers that Ila is pregnant and vows to kill her child if it is a girl. Shem and Ila build a raft to escape Noah, but he discovers it and burns it.

Eventually Tubal-Cain emerges from his hiding place and attempts to kill Noah. But Ham stabs him with a dagger before he can push Noah overboard. Ila gives birth to twin girls, but when Noah hears her singing lullabies to the newborns, he cannot go through with his murderous plan.

For those wondering which of the movie's plot points and details align with the biblical account of Noah, here is a quick summary:

- Noah was the grandson of Methuselah.
- He had three sons.
- He built an ark. ∎

Left: Logan Lerman and Russell Crowe in the film *Noah* (2014).
Above Right: Russell Crowe as Noah in the film *Noah* (2014).

Above: *Noah* movie poster (2014).

76 When the Game Stands Tall

Based on an inspiring true story, *When the Game Stands Tall* introduces Bob Ladouceur, the head football coach of the De La Salle (California) Spartans, whose teams won a record 151 games in a row from 1992 to 2004. Ladouceur is more than a football coach; he's also a molder of character.

As the religious instructor in the school, Ladouceur makes frequent use of the Bible and its teachings, in and out of the locker room. Twice in the movie, the Spartan team is depicted saying the Lord's Prayer from Matthew 6:9–13. In another scene, Coach Ladouceur invites his players to share their thoughts on the meaning of Luke 6:38 ("Give, and it will be given to you"). Their replies offer insight into their feelings about God. Jesus's words in Matthew 23:12 ("Whoever exalts himself will be humbled, and whoever humbles himself will be exalted") are discussed and applied. A gravestone quotes James 4:10.

These Bible quotes provide comfort and encouragement as Coach Ladouceur and his team struggle to work through the terminal illness of a player's mother, the sudden death of another player, and the end of their vaunted winning streak. ∎

Top Right: Jim Caviezel, Alexander Ludwig, and Michael Chiklis in the film *When the Game Stands Tall* (2014).
Above: Scene from the film *When the Game Stands Tall* (2014).

77 Stranger in a Strange Land

Robert A. Heinlein

In this science-fiction classic, Valentine Michael Smith, the first human born and raised on Mars, returns to Earth, where various political factions and religious groups vie to use him for their own purposes. Possessed with extraordinary powers, "Mike" begins to spread a message of love that attracts many followers. Not everyone responds to his message, however. At the end of the novel, Mike is killed by an angry mob. After he ascends to heaven to become an archangel, his followers continue spreading his message on earth.

Author Robert A. Heinlein suggests some unmistakable parallels (and, in some cases, distinctions) between Mike and Jesus—some of which might be more accurately described as parodies. The title of part 1 of the book is "His Maculate Conception." Unlike Jesus, Mike was conceived by two human parents, albeit on another planet.

Like Jesus, Mike ultimately rejects the opportunity to wield political power and chooses to address people's spiritual needs. However, occasionally Mike uses his supernatural powers to cause harm to his enemies by making them disappear. In contrast, in the Bible, Jesus uses his supernatural powers only to bring comfort and healing to others.

In the book, Mike is familiar with the Bible and makes numerous references to Bible characters and stories, such as Lot and Elisha.

Though the content of their messages and their relationships with their disciples differ significantly, both Mike and Jesus are killed by their opponents. Both ascend to heaven. Both of their missions are continued by their followers. ■

Right: Landscape of the night sky by Denis Belitsky.
Top: Martian landscape art created by Jurik Peter.

78 The Lion, the Witch, and the Wardrobe
C. S. Lewis

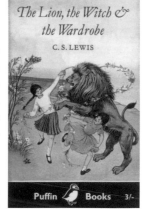

In C. S. Lewis's biblical allegory, four siblings—Peter, Susan, Edmund, and Lucy—discover a passageway inside an enormous wardrobe that leads them to the land of Narnia. In Narnia, they encounter friendly creatures such as Mr. Tumnus the fawn and Mr. Beaver. Edmund encounters the evil White Witch, who turns him against the others. Most significantly, they meet Aslan the lion, the king of Narnia.

After Tumnus is imprisoned by the White Witch, the children travel with Mr. Beaver to enlist Aslan's help. Edmund breaks from the group to warn the White Witch of Aslan's arrival. Rather than being grateful for his help, the witch prepares to kill Edmund.

Aslan and his followers rescue Edmund in the nick of time. However, the White Witch informs Aslan that according to the laws of Narnia, Edmund must be put to death for being a traitor. Aslan strikes a deal with the witch that seems to satisfy her, and she releases Edmund.

The next day, as Susan and Lucy look on from a hiding place, Aslan allows the White Witch and her followers to torment and eventually kill him. He gives his life for Edmund's.

Aslan doesn't stay dead long, though. The next morning, he rises again and leads the children and his followers in an epic battle against the White Witch. Aslan eventually kills the witch and defeats her forces, which parallels the prophecies in Revelation 16:16–20 of what is commonly called the Battle of Armageddon.

Aslan stands as one of the best-known and best-loved messianic figures in all of literature. His sacrificial death and subsequent return to life have obvious parallels in the crucifixion and resurrection of Jesus, as recorded in the Gospels. ∎

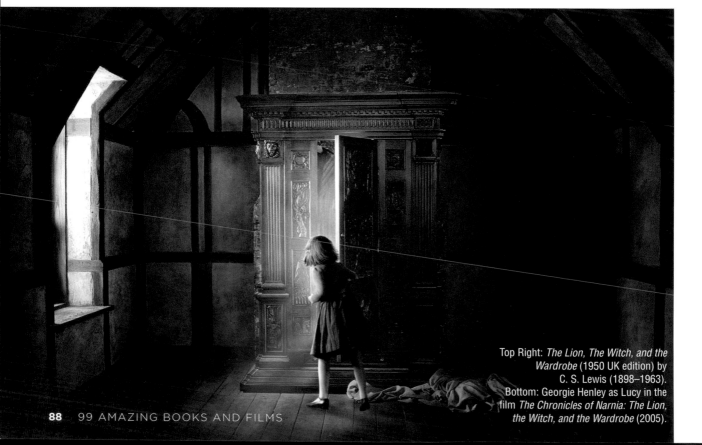

Top Right: *The Lion, The Witch, and the Wardrobe* (1950 UK edition) by C. S. Lewis (1898–1963).
Bottom: Georgie Henley as Lucy in the film *The Chronicles of Narnia: The Lion, the Witch, and the Wardrobe* (2005).

79 Great Expectations

In director David Lean's adaptation of Charles Dickens's timeless classic *Great Expectations*—generally regarded as one of the greatest films in the history of British cinema—Bibles serve as indicators of the spiritual condition of various characters. For example, Abel Magwitch, the fearsome criminal, becomes the secret benefactor of Pip, the film's protagonist. Magwitch carries with him a "greasy little clasped black Testament" (as it's described in the novel). But the purpose of this Bible isn't encouragement or spiritual growth. Instead, the Testament is a tool of Magwitch's trade, something for people to swear on, as needed.

Mr. Wopsle's great-aunt uses three tattered Bibles as reading primers in her classroom. She sees practical uses for the book rather than spiritual ones.

Miss Havisham's *Book of Common Prayer*, a Bible supplement of sorts, is seen among her discarded possessions. Its abandonment is a sad commentary on a spiritual journey that never reached a meaningful conclusion. ■

Top: Anthony Wager in the film *Great Expectations* (1946).   Right: Scene from the film *Great Expectations* (1946).

1962

1919-114

80 To Kill a Mockingbird

The fifth commandment that God gave Moses and the Hebrew people in the book of Exodus—"Honor your father and your mother" (Exodus 20:12)—is one of the themes in the film adaptation of Harper Lee's beloved novel. Atticus Finch, surely the noblest lawyer in all of literature and film, is a single father to Jem and Scout (whose given name is Jean Louise), two precocious children in Maycomb, Alabama, in 1932. The film is narrated by the adult Scout, who looks back lovingly on the father whose values helped shape her.

An even larger theme is racism and partiality. Atticus can be said to represent the impartial, non-racist attitude of God, based on Acts 10:34: "God shows no partiality."

As the film's racially charged narrative unfolds, Jem and Scout begin to recognize the full scope of their father's dignity, compassion, and courage, as well as his sense of honor and duty. When a black man named Tom Robinson is accused of raping a white woman, Atticus agrees to defend him, despite threats and intimidation from people in his community.

His bold stand threatens the white status quo. It also resonates powerfully through Maycomb's downtrodden black community. During the trial, Scout sits with members of that community in the gallery balcony.

To no one's surprise, the jury finds Robinson guilty. Atticus reassures his client that they stand a good chance to win an appeal and then starts to gather his things. The African American townspeople in the gallery wait for him. As he leaves the courtroom, they all rise to their feet in a heartfelt show of respect. One of them, Reverend Sykes, nudges Scout and says, "Miss Jean Louise, stand up. Your father's passin'."[24] ∎

Top: Gregory Peck as a lawyer in the film *To Kill a Mockingbird* (1962).

 # 81 One Flew Over the Cuckoo's Nest

Randle McMurphy, the central character of Ken Kesey's novel and Miloš Forman's Academy Award–winning movie, stands as another in a long line of messianic figures in literature and film. As the movie opens, McMurphy is admitted to a mental institution after having himself declared insane. Convicted of a minor offense, he plans to avoid prison labor by spending his sentence in the relative comfort of the institution.

He soon comes to regret his decision.

McMurphy's presence changes the dynamic of the psychiatric ward immediately. His bold and rebellious personality clashes with that of the repressed and manipulative Nurse Ratched, who rules the ward with an iron fist.

Many other patients on the ward quickly warm up to McMurphy and begin to look to him for guidance and leadership, not unlike disciples. When McMurphy discovers that most of them are there on a voluntary basis and can leave whenever they like, he encourages them to pursue their freedom. He shows them a new way of thinking—a path to salvation. McMurphy makes several explicit references to the Bible, such as his remark that Bibbit should be a "fisher of men" (Matthew 4:19; Mark 1:17), his fishing trip with twelve men (or disciples), and his description of the electroshock conductant as "a crown of thorns" (John 19:2, 5).

In the end, though, McMurphy pays for his radicalism. He is lobotomized and later killed. ∎

Above: Danny DeVito, Jack Nicholson, Brad Dourif, and William Redfield in the film *One Flew Over the Cuckoo's Nest* (1975).

82 Being There

An ANDREW BRAUNSBERG Production of a HAL ASHBY film

Peter Sellers   Shirley MacLaine

BEING THERE

Being There *is a gentle comic fantasy film* masquerading as a political satire. Peter Sellers plays Chance, a simple-minded gardener whose employer/father figure dies, leaving him with no place to live and no way to fend for himself. Though Chance is middle-aged, he's had virtually no contact with the world outside the townhouse where he lived with the man who found him as a baby on his doorstep and raised him as his own. Almost everything Chance knows and says comes from television.

With no place to go, Chance wanders around Washington, DC, befuddled by the workings of the city. His destiny changes when he is struck by a car belonging to Ben Rand, a wealthy businessman with friends in the highest of places.

Ben is intrigued by Chance, whose name he mistakenly believes is Chauncey Gardiner. He interprets Chance's banal description of lawyers kicking him out of his townhouse as transparency of his business ventures and comes to believe that Chance is a high-powered corporate executive.

This sets the tone for the film's narrative. As Chance is introduced to Ben's elite circle of acquaintances, including several high-ranking government officials, his simplistic utterings about gardening and the weather are taken as deep political and philosophical insights. The simplicity of his words evidence his wisdom.

For those who miss the allusion to Jesus, director Hal Ashby saves his most striking image for last. After Ben dies, and his pallbearers offer the name Chauncey Gardiner as a potential candidate for the presidency, Chance wanders away through Ben's garden. When he comes to a small lake, he steps onto its surface and continues across, literally walking on water—recalling the story of Jesus as described in Matthew 14:25. ■

Above Left: *Being There* original movie poster (1979).

 Est of Eden

83 East of Eden

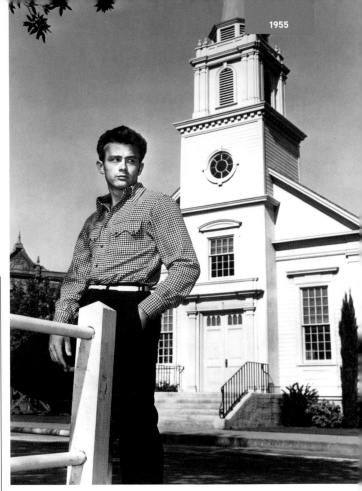

1955

In Elia Kazan's film* East of Eden, *loosely based on John Steinbeck's landmark novel of the same name, the Genesis story of Cain and Abel echoes across two generations of the deeply dysfunctional Trask family in early twentieth-century Mendocino, California. Elia Kazan's film adaptation of the novel focuses on only one generation.

Adam Trask is a successful farmer and the chairman of the local draft board—a key position while World War I rages in Europe. In the parallels to the Cain and Abel story, Adam represents not just his biblical namesake but also God himself. His twin sons, Cal and Aron, represent Cain and Abel, respectively.

Cal is a tortured soul, desperate to please his father but never able to do so. Aron, on the other hand, is the apple of his father's eye—a fact that adds to Cal's anguish and drives a wedge between the brothers.

Both boys have been told that their mother died, but Cal learns that she actually runs a brothel in a nearby town. After Adam loses his fortune to a bad investment, Cal borrows five thousand dollars from his mother to start his own business venture. He makes enough money to recoup his father's losses. However, when he presents the money to his father as a gift, Adam accuses him of war profiteering and refuses to take it.

Stung by yet another rejection, as well as Adam's undeniable favoritism toward Aron, Cal makes a rash decision to tell—or rather, show—Aron the truth about their mother. Aron is so devastated that he immediately enlists in the Army and boards a troop train. Before Adam can stop him, the train pulls away.

The local sheriff, aware of what Cal has done, connects him to his biblical counterpart (the inspiration for Steinbeck's title) by paraphrasing Genesis 4:8 and 16, which say, "Cain rose up against Abel his brother, and slew him. . . . And Cain went out from the presence of the LORD, and dwelt in the land of Nod, on the east of Eden" (KJV).

"Why don't you go away, Cal," the sheriff suggests.[25]

Like Abel, Aron is killed—not at the hands of his brother, but in combat. The stress proves too much for Adam, who suffers a paralyzing stroke. Cal, unlike Cain in the Genesis account, manages to reconcile with his father before his father dies. ∎

Top Right: James Dean as Cal in the film *East of Eden* (1955).
Above Left: Richard Davalos, James Dean, and Julie Harris in the film *East of Eden* (1955).

84 Lord of the Flies
William Golding

Depictions of Satan have been pervasive in art and literature. For example, William Golding's classic novel *Lord of the Flies* took its name from Mark 3:22, where a demon is called Beelzebul, which can mean "lord of the flies." Beelzebul (or Beelzebub) is an alternative name for Satan.

In Golding's novel, a group of boys is being evacuated by air during wartime. When their plane crashes on a desert island, they attempt to govern themselves—with disastrous consequences. The barbaric nature of the boys is driven home by their act of killing a sow and placing its decapitated head on a stake. Originally intended as a sacrifice to the monster they believe stalks the island, the sow's head—the "Lord of the Flies"—comes to embody the evil that settles over the group.

Flies have also been used in films to portray demonic forces. One example is *The Green Mile*, based on Stephen King's novel of the same name. John, one of the main characters, is a falsely accused jail inmate who seems to have the ability to heal others with his supernatural powers. As he "heals" people, it appears that swarms of flies come out of them and are ingested by John. This visual image is similar to descriptions of Jesus casting out demons in the Gospels. ∎

Above: Hugh Edwards and James Aubrey in the film *Lord of the Flies* (1963).

85 Blade Runner

Blade Runner is set in a bleak future—a world in which synthetic humans known as Replicants are used for manual labor on off-world colonies. Rick Deckard, the "blade runner" of the title, is assigned to hunt down four Replicants who have come back to earth to find their creator.

Ridley Scott's groundbreaking science-fiction classic, based on the short story "Do Androids Dream of Electric Sheep?" by Phillip K. Dick, contains a subtle biblical subtext that serves to deepen its characters and its narrative.

J. F. Sebastian, a genetic designer of the Replicants, symbolizes Jesus in the film. Many people believe the New Testament teaches that Jesus chose to live among humans, even though he is God. In the film, Sebastian chooses to live among the Replicants, even though he is human. Jesus's purpose in the Gospels, according to some people, is to reunite humanity with the Creator. Sebastian's quest in the film is to reunite the Replicant Batty with his creator. Both Jesus and Sebastian are murdered for their efforts.

Sebastian is not the only character in the film whose actions are reminiscent of Jesus. The Replicant Batty drives a nail through his own hand in an unmistakably symbolic gesture. It is that nail-scarred hand that later saves Deckard. ■

Top: Scene from the film *Blade Runner* (1982). Above Right: Spacecraft in the futuristic film *Blade Runner* (1982).

86

ABSALOM! ABSALOM!

William Faulkner

William Faulkner's novel Absalom! Absalom! immediately suggests a biblical theme by its title. In the Bible, Absalom was the third son of David, king of Israel. Absalom's story can be found in 2 Samuel 13–18. In these chapters we find out how Absalom, in an attempt to avenge his sister Tamar, carried out a plan to murder his half brother Amnon. To avoid having to face his father, Absalom fled Jerusalem. Recognized for his "handsome appearance" (2 Samuel 14:25), Absalom gained the

support of the people of Israel and unlawfully proclaimed himself as king.

Absalom's relationship with his father deteriorated, and David often feared his own son. But David gave orders for his soldiers to "deal gently" with Absalom and "protect" him (2 Samuel 18:5, 12). Ignoring the order, Joab, the king's commander, thrust three javelins into Absalom's heart when Absalom's hair got tangled in a tree during a brutal battle. Absalom died after Joab's armor-bearers "struck him and killed him" (2 Samuel 18:15). When David heard about his son's death, he was so distraught that he wailed, "O my son Absalom, my son, my son Absalom! Would I had died instead of you, O Absalom, my son, my son!" (2 Samuel 18:33).

In Faulkner's *Absalom! Absalom!*—set in the time of the American Civil War—Henry Sutpen, the son of Thomas Sutpen, seeks to protect his sister Judith by killing his half brother Charles Bon. ■

Top Right: 1954 portrait of William Faulkner (1897–1962) by Carl Van Vechten (1880–1964).
Above: Rowan Oak, built in 1844, was the home of author William Faulkner.

87 The Green Mile

John Coffey (note the initials) is a gentle giant. He is also an African American man in the Deep South in 1935, falsely accused of raping and murdering two little girls. Yet there is much more to the man than his temperament and legal predicament.

As he waits on Death Row, known as "the Green Mile," John Coffey demonstrates a remarkable ability. He can cure illness and disease by placing his hands on a suffering person. He heals an excruciating bladder infection in Paul Edgecomb, one of the guards on the Mile. When a fellow prisoner's beloved pet mouse is stomped to death, Coffey brings it back to life. And when it is discovered that the warden's wife is suffering from a brain tumor, Paul and his fellow guards sneak Coffey out of the prison and take him to the warden's home to remove the tumor.

Similar to the story of Jesus in the Gospels, in this story an innocent person—whose mission was to bring love and healing to the world and who possessed extraordinary healing powers for that purpose—is put to death for crimes he did not commit.

Frank Darabont's adaptation of the serialized novel by Stephen King is justifiably recognized as a "statement film" regarding the death penalty. But it also contains some unmistakable and vivid Bible imagery. ■

Above Left: Tom Hanks as Paul Edgecomb in the film *The Green Mile* (1999).
Right: Michael Clarke Duncan in the film *The Green Mile* (1999).

88 The Magnificent Seven

This remake of the classic 1960 Western (which itself was a remake of the landmark 1954 Japanese film *The Seven Samurai*) tells the story of seven men who agree to defend a small town against an army hired by an evil industrialist. The men train the townspeople to assist them in protecting their homes and families and turning away those who seek to take everything from them.

The 2016 remake incorporates several Bible references that are not found in the original. On the night before the big battle, the townspeople gather for a prayer service. The priest leading the service reminds the people of Jesus's words as recorded in Matthew 18:20: "For where two or three are gathered together in my name, there am I in the midst of them" (KJV).

Some characters pray the Lord's Prayer from Matthew 6:9–13 before the battle begins. Jack Horne, one of the titular Seven, quotes Psalm 23:4: "Though I walk through the valley of the shadow of death, I will fear no evil: for thou art with me" (KJV). ∎

Top: Promotional shot for the film *The Magnificent Seven* (2016).

89

Spider-Man

"With great power comes great responsibility"[26]
Those words, spoken to Peter Parker (alias Spider-Man) by his Uncle Ben, serve as an inspiration, guiding principle, and haunting reminder for the young web slinger—especially after his uncle is killed by a street thug whom Spider-Man failed to apprehend.

Compare Uncle Ben's words of wisdom to the depiction of Jesus's teaching in Luke 12:48, which might be summarized as "To whom much is given, much is expected," and you get a glimpse at a key source of inspiration for Spider-Man's creators.

The Bible's influence on the 2002 summer blockbuster is more clearly revealed in an action sequence later in the movie. After Spider-Man's archenemy, the Green Goblin, discovers Spidey's secret identity, he sets out to destroy everything Spider-Man/Peter Parker holds dear, including his Aunt May (the widow of Uncle Ben). As she is being attacked, Aunt May prays the Lord's Prayer, word for word, as it is written in Matthew 6:9–13. ∎

Above Right: Willem Dafoe as the Green Goblin in the film *Spider-Man* (2002).   Above: *Spider-Man* movie poster (2002).   **99**

90

The Birth of a Nation

Nate Parker's critically acclaimed directorial debut weaves Bible references and context throughout the story of Nat Turner, the preacher-slave who led a violent revolt against plantation owners in Virginia in 1831. Parker also stars as Turner, a man torn between his spiritual calling and his recognition of the need for action.

The Bible figures prominently in Turner's life. As a young boy, he is taught to read using the Bible ("the best book ever written,"[27] as it is described to him). Later he becomes a pastor and engages in a debate with a white minister over whether the Bible supports slavery. Turner is whipped for espousing his beliefs regarding the Bible's stand.

In time, Turner begins to see himself as part of a long line of freedom fighters—one whose ranks include the leaders David, Gideon, Joshua, and Samson. ■

Above: Nate Parker and Aja Naomi King in the film *Birth of a Nation* (2016).

91 Footloose

In this remake of the beloved 1980s classic, Ren, a teenage newcomer to the town of Bomont, fights to get the town's ban on public dancing lifted. To do that, he must take on Reverend Moore, the local minister and community leader—and father of Ariel, whom Ren loves.

The Bible figures prominently, not just in the controversy but also in the lives of various characters. When Reverend Moore tells Ariel to stay away from Ren because he's trouble, she responds by quoting Job 14:1: "Man who is born of a woman is few of days and full of trouble."

Ariel helps Ren prepare a speech to convince the city council to lift the ban—a speech that includes no fewer than three Bible verses that they believe support dancing:

- "Let them praise his name with dancing, making melody to him with tambourine and lyre!" (Psalm 149:3).
- "And David danced before the LORD with all his might" (2 Samuel 6:14).
- "A time to weep, and a time to laugh; a time to mourn, and a time to dance" (Ecclesiastes 3:4).

In the end, dance cannot be stopped. Reverend Moore relaxes his stance, and the movie concludes with a joyous celebration filled with rhythmic movement set to music. ∎

Right: Kenny Wormald (right) as Ren in the film *Footloose* (2011).
Top: Julianne Hough (center) and Kenny Wormald (right of center) in the film *Footloose* (2011).

92 The Prince of Egypt

This animated retelling of the Hebrew Exodus from Egypt delves deeply into the relationships between Moses and his adopted Egyptian family. The Bible offers few insights into these relationships, so it's left to the screenwriters of *The Prince of Egypt* to suggest the following:

- Moses and his half brother Rameses (the future pharaoh) were vandals who damaged a temple under renovation during a reckless chariot race.
- Pharaoh Seti named Rameses the Prince Regent of Egypt because of Moses's encouragement.
- Zipporah, Moses's wife, was given to him by Rameses after she nearly attacked the young Egyptian regent.
- Rameses named Moses the Royal Chief Architect of Egypt.
- Moses encountered his Hebrew siblings, Miriam and Aaron, in the desert while he was following Zipporah after her escape—and there learned his true identity.
- Miriam predicted that Moses would lead the Hebrews out of Egypt.
- Rameses witnessed Moses's killing of the Egyptian overseer and offered to help him cover it up.
- A camel saved Moses's life in the desert.
- Zipporah (and not Aaron) accompanied Moses on his first confrontation with Pharaoh Rameses.

The Prince of Egypt covers the biblical narrative from the birth of Moses to the giving of the Ten Commandments. The film ends with Moses descending from the mountain, holding two tablets inscribed with the Ten Commandments. The first part of the journey is over, but the adventure is just beginning. ∎

TWO BROTHERS
UNITED BY FRIENDSHIP
DIVIDED BY DESTINY

THE PRINCE OF EGYPT

www.prince-of-egypt.com

December 18, 1998

DREAMWORKS
PICTURES

Right: *The Prince of Egypt* advance movie poster (1998).

93

Amazing Grace

The film opens in 1796 with British Parliament member William Wilberforce recalling his career in politics—specifically, his fruitless fifteen-year struggle to introduce legislation that would abolish slave trade in the British Empire. As the title implies, *Amazing Grace* is not just a historical drama or an examination of British politics in the eighteenth century.

A moment of spiritual enlightenment is cited as the driving force behind Wilberforce's abolitionist efforts. In fact, after aligning himself with the evangelical arm of the Church of England, Wilberforce's first instinct is to give up politics altogether and devote himself to Christian ministry and outreach. His friends in Parliament, however, convince him that he can do more good as a politician.

Even more persuasive is the input of his former mentor, John Newton, a man haunted by his tenure as a slave ship captain and overwhelmed by the forgiveness promised to him in the Bible. Newton claims the promise in 1 John 1:9 ("If we confess our sins, he is faithful and just to forgive us our sins and to cleanse us from all unrighteousness") with one simple declaration: "Although my memory's fading, I remember two things very clearly. I'm a great sinner and Christ is a great Savior."[28] From that overwhelming sense of spiritual gratitude and astonishment, Newton composed the poem that would become the title hymn.

Opposed by powerful corporate interests, Wilberforce's campaign takes a dreadful toll on his health. Still, he perseveres. And in 1807, after two decades of political maneuvering, Wilberforce introduces a bill that finally abolishes slave trade in the British Empire. ■

Above: Youssou N'Dour and Ioan Gruffudd in the film *Amazing Grace* (2006).

94 Pulp Fiction

Quentin Tarantino's landmark second film won the Palme d'Or, the highest prize awarded at the 1994 Cannes Film Festival, and was nominated for seven Academy Awards. The American Film Institute ranks it ninety-four on the list of the greatest American movies.

The movie contains three interrelated stories involving mobsters and small-time criminals. Jules Winnfield (Samuel L. Jackson) and Vincent Vega (John Travolta) figure prominently in two of those stories as hitmen. Jules and Vincent are (necessarily, by virtue of their profession) daunting, unnerving figures. They are also supremely self-aware.

To burnish his reputation as one who must be feared, Jules uses a Bible passage. Before he executes his victims, he recites—with deep gravitas and gun pointed—a rather dramatic embellishment of Ezekiel 25:17. To quote Jules:

The path of the righteous man is beset on all sides by the inequities of the selfish and the tyranny of evil men. Blessed is he who, in the name of charity and good will, shepherds the weak through the valley of darkness, for he is truly his brother's keeper and the finder of lost children. And I will strike down upon thee with great vengeance and furious anger those who attempt to poison and destroy my brothers. And you will know my name is the Lord when I lay my vengeance upon you.[29]

In the final scene of the movie, Jules attempts to interpret the verse as it relates to him, his victims, and the people he imagines that he shepherds. ■

Top: John Travolta as a hitman in the film *Pulp Fiction* (1994).

95 Evan Almighty

In this comic sequel to Bruce Almighty, anchorman-turned-congressman Evan Baxter (Steve Carell) is tapped by God (Morgan Freeman) to build a modern-day ark.

After the newly elected Baxter arrives in Washington, he is pressured to cosponsor a bill in Congress that would allow corporate development in national parks. That's when strange things start happening. Animals follow him wherever he goes. His beard grows to presumed biblical proportions—immediately after he shaves. Building supplies—the kind described in the Hebrew Bible—are sent to his house. The number 614—a reference to Genesis 6:14, in which God instructs Noah to build an ark—appears wherever he looks.

Taking the hints, Baxter resigns himself to the task and begins the construction of an enormous ark. He endures the ridicule of the press and the doubts of his family to complete the task. And then he waits for the downpour.

The Genesis account of Noah's ark is tweaked and parodied throughout the film. In the end, the deluge is caused not by a rainstorm but by the collapse of a poorly designed dam—one sponsored by the same congressman who pressured Baxter earlier.

Thanks to Baxter's ark, the animals on board, along with Baxter's family and the media who had gathered to interview him, are spared. ■

96 Harry Potter and the Deathly Hallows: Part 2

The biblical allusions scattered throughout the *Harry Potter* saga—the wicked serpent, the enemy who fell from grace—build to their logical conclusion in the climax of the final film in the original series.

The showdown between Dumbledore's army and Voldemort's forces of evil is at hand. Voldemort warns that unless Harry gives himself up to die, everyone who

stands with him will be killed. Harry's response calls to mind Jesus's words in John 15:13: "Greater love has no one than this, that someone lay down his life for his friends." That's exactly what Harry does.

He goes alone to the Forbidden Forest, where Voldemort kills him with a curse. He sacrifices his own life in order to save others.

The parallels to Jesus's story in the Bible don't stop there. After spending some time with the already deceased Dumbledore in a place that resembles heaven, Harry's consciousness returns to his lifeless body in the Forbidden Forest. He later stuns his friends, followers, and enemies by rising from the dead.

After his resurrection, Harry engages in one final, epic battle with his nemesis. And when the last magic spell is cast, the evil Lord Voldemort is vanquished for good. ■

Above Left: Daniel Radcliffe and Ralph Fiennes in the film *Harry Potter and the Deathly Hallows: Part 2* (2011).
Top: Daniel Radcliffe as Harry Potter in the film *Harry Potter and the Deathly Hallows: Part 2* (2011).

97

Soul Surfer

Soul Surfer *tells the inspiring true-life story* of Bethany Hamilton, a teenage competitive surfer in Hawaii who loses her left arm in a tiger shark attack. Convinced that her surfing career is over, Bethany falls into a funk until a church missions trip to tsunami-ravaged Thailand helps her put her loss in perspective.

To help a young Thai boy overcome his fear of water, Bethany uses her surfboard. And that's when she realizes that she can use her gift to help others. Her passion for surfing reignited, Bethany begins training again. Invited to compete in the national championship, she comes tantalizingly close to winning before finishing in third place.

References to Bethany's Christian faith abound in the film. The Bible is quoted twice. The first occurs at a youth group meeting Bethany attends before the attack. In a bit of foreshadowing, the youth pastor shares God's words of inspiration in Jeremiah 29:11: "For I know the plans I have for you . . . plans to prosper you and not to harm you, plans to give you hope and a future" (NIV).

The second occurs in Bethany's hospital room, shortly after the attack. When Bethany asks when she can start surfing again, her father offers encouragement by paraphrasing the words found in Philippians 4:13: "You can do all things through him who gives you strength."[30] ∎

Left: AnnaSophia Robb as Bethany Hamilton in the film *Soul Surfer* (2011).
Above: Water image created by Yeryomina Anastassiya.

98 Left Behind

Two men will be in the field; one will be taken and the other left. Two women will be grinding at the mill; one will be taken and one left. Therefore, stay awake, for you do not know on what day your Lord is coming. But know this, that if the master of the house had known in what part of the night the thief was coming, he would have stayed awake and would not have let his house be broken into. Therefore you also must be ready, for the Son of Man is coming at an hour you do not expect. (Matthew 24:40–44)

Many Christians believe the scenario in this Bible passage refers to the Rapture—an end-times event when Christians believe they will be reunited with Jesus. This plays out on a global scale in this apocalyptic thriller based on the best-selling book series by Tim LaHaye and Jerry Jenkins.

Rayford Steele is an airline pilot who must find a way to land his plane when his copilot, a crew member, and several passengers suddenly disappear midflight, leaving their clothes and possessions behind. While trying to quiet the panic aboard the plane, Steele struggles to establish radio contact with the ground. His only hope is to try to get back to New York before the plane runs out of fuel.

On the ground in New York, his daughter, Chloe, a college student, tries to make her way through the chaos that results when hundreds of thousands of people throughout the city suddenly disappear. Eventually she encounters a church pastor who explains that the world's Christians have been taken to heaven. Those left behind, including himself—

he admits that he didn't truly believe what he preached—will be forced to deal with a new universal reality.

With Chloe's help, Rayford lands the plane safely on a bridge that is under construction. When the remaining passengers disembark, however, the scene before them looks frighteningly like the end of the world—mirroring the apocalyptic events the writers believe are prophesied in the Bible. ■

NICOLAS CAGE
ASHLEY TISDALE
CHAD MICHAEL MURRAY

FROM DIRECTOR VIC ARMSTRONG

SOME WERE SAVED, AND SOME WERE...

LEFT BEHIND

Arclight films

Right: *Left Behind* movie poster (2014).

99 Pinocchio

The story of Jonah has made its way into numerous films. Among them is the 1940 Disney animated classic *Pinocchio*. It tells the story of the puppet Pinocchio, who is on a journey to become a real boy. One of his many adventures is being swallowed by Monstro the whale. Like Jonah, Pinocchio survives.

Disney released another, lesser-known cartoon called *The Whalers* in 1938. In it, Mickey Mouse, Donald Duck, and Goofy are the crew of a whaling ship. In a series of mishaps, Goofy, like Jonah, finds himself alive inside a whale. He escapes after lighting a match inside, which causes the whale to sneeze.

Among the more modern examples is the children's series *VeggieTales*, which used humanlike vegetable characters to depict Bible stories. The film *Jonah: A VeggieTales Movie* was released in 2002 and was nominated for an Annie Award, a prestigious award for animated films. ■

Above: Scene from the animated film *Pinocchio* (1940).

References

1. Michael Sassone (as Preacher Purl), *Hoosiers*, written by Angelo Pizzo, directed by David Anspaugh (November 14, 1986; Hemdale Pictures, De Haven Productions/Orion Pictures); "Hoosiers Quotes," IMDb, accessed July 16, 2017, http://www.imdb.com/title/tt0091217/quotes.

2. Shia LaBeouf (as Boyd "Bible" Swan), *Fury*, written and directed by David Ayer (October 15, 2014; Le Grisbi Productions, QED International, LStar Capital, Crave Films, Plan B/Columbia Pictures); "Fury Quotes," IMDb, accessed July 16, 2017, http://www.imdb.com/title/tt2713180/quotes.

3. Brad Pitt (as Don "Wardaddy" Collier), *Fury*, written and directed by David Ayer (October 15, 2014; Le Grisbi Productions, QED International, LStar Capital, Crave Films, Plan B/Columbia Pictures); "Fury Quotes," IMDb, accessed July 16, 2017, http://www.imdb.com/title/tt2713180/quotes.

4. Ibid.

5. Shia LaBeouf (as Boyd "Bible" Swan), *Fury*, written and directed by David Ayer (October 15, 2014; Le Grisbi Productions, QED International, LStar Capital, Crave Films, Plan B/Columbia Pictures);"Fury Quotes," IMDb, accessed July 16, 2017, http://www.imdb.com/title/tt2713180/quotes.

6. Bob Gunton (as Warden Norton), *The Shawshank Redemption*, directed by Frank Darabont (September 10, 1994; Castle Rock Entertainment/Columbia Pictures).

7. *The Shawshank Redemption*, directed by Frank Darabont (September 10, 1994; Castle Rock Entertainment/Columbia Pictures).

8. Joseph Heller, *Catch-22: A Novel* (New York: Simon and Schuster, 1999), 60.

9. Ibid., 89.

10. Ibid.

11. Karl Malden (as Father Barry), *On the Waterfront*, directed by Elia Kazan (July 28, 1954, Horizon Pictures/Columbia Pictures).

12. Ibid.

13. Marlon Brando (as Sky Masterson), *Guys and Dolls*, directed by Joseph L. Mankiewicz(New York: November 3, 1955; Samuel Goldwyn Productions/Metro-Goldwyn-Mayer).

14. Ibid.

15. Max von Sydow (as Antonius Block), *The Seventh Seal*, directed by Ingmar Bergman (October 13, 1958; AB Svensk Filmindustri).

16. Orson Welles (as Cardinal Wolsey), *A Man for All Seasons*, directed by Fred Zinnemann (New York: December 12, 1966; Highland Films/Columbia Pictures).

17. Paul Scofield (as Sir Thomas More), *A Man for All Seasons*, directed by Fred Zinnemann (New York: December 12, 1966; Highland Films/Columbia Pictures).

18. Brember Wills (as Saul Femm), *The Old Dark House*, directed by James Whale (October 20, 1932; Universal Pictures).

19. Richard Frank (as Father Vogler), *Amadeus*, directed by Miloš Forman (Los Angeles: September 6, 1984; The Saul Zaentz Company).

20. F. Murray Abraham (as Antonio Salieri), *Amadeus*, directed by Miloš Forman (Los Angeles: September 6, 1984; The Saul Zaentz Company).

21. Jarl Kulle (as General Lorens Löwenhielm), *Babette's Feast*, directed by Gabriel Axel (March 4, 1988; Nordisk Film).

22. Robert Prosky (as Father John Cavanaugh), *Rudy*, directed by David Anspaugh (October 13, 1993; TriStar Pictures).

23. Barry Pepper (as Private Daniel Jackson), *Saving Private Ryan*, directed by Steven Spielberg (July 24, 1998; Amblin Entertainment, Mutual Film Company/DreamWorks Pictures).

24. William "Bill" Walker (as Reverend Sykes), *To Kill a Mockingbird*, directed by Robert Mulligan (December 25, 1962; Brentwood Productions, Pakula-Mullian/Universal Pictures).

25. Burl Ives (as Sam the Sheriff), *East of Eden*, directed by Elia Kazan (New York: March 9, 1955; Warner Bros.).

26. Cliff Robertson (as Ben Parker), *Spider-Man*, directed by Sam Raimi (April 29, 2002; Marvel Enterprises, Arthur Coburn/Columbia Pictures).

27. *The Birth of a Nation*, directed by Nate Parker (January 25, 2016; Bron Studios, Mandalay Pictures, Phantom Four, Tiny Giant Entertainment/Fox Searchlight Pictures).

28. Albert Finney (as John Newton), *Amazing Grace*, directed by Michael Apted (TIFF: September 16, 2006; FourBoys Films, Walden Media, Bristol Bay Productions, Ingenious Film Partners, Roadside Attractions/Momentum Pictures, Samuel Goldwyn Films).

29. Samuel L. Jackson (as Jules Winnfield), *Pulp Fiction*, directed by Quentin Tarantino (May 12, 1994; A Band Apart, Jersey Films/Miramax Films).

30. Dennis Quaid (as Tom Hamilton), *Soul Surfer*, directed by Sean McNamara (April 8, 2011; Mandalay Vision, Brookwell McNamara Entertainment, Island Film Group, Enticing Entertainment, Affirm Films, Life's a Beach Entertainment/TriStar Pictures, FilmDistrict).

museum of the Bible

Experience the Book
that Shapes History

Museum of the Bible is a 430,000-square-foot building located in the heart of Washington, D.C.—just steps from the National Mall and the U.S. Capitol. Displaying artifacts from several collections, the Museum explores the Bible's history, narrative and impact through high-tech exhibits, immersive settings, and interactive experiences. Upon entering, you pass through two massive, bronze gates resembling printing plates from Genesis 1. Beyond the gates, an incredible replica of an ancient artifact containing Psalm 19 hangs behind etched glass panels. Come be inspired by the imagination and innovation used to display thousands of years of biblical history.

Museum of the Bible aims to be the most technologically advanced museum in the world, starting with its unique Digital Guide that allows guests to personalize their museum experience with navigation, customized tours, supplemental visual and audio content, and more.

**For more information and to plan your visit, go to
museumoftheBible.org.**